BEHAVIOURAL DISORDERS IN CHILDREN AND ADULTS

A Fresh Perspective

Insight—Empathy—Treatment

GEERTJE POST UITERWEER

TRANSLATED FROM THE DUTCH BY EDELINE LEFEVRE

TEMPLE LODGE

Publisher's Note
The information in this book is not intended to be taken as a replacement for medical advice. Any person with a condition requiring medical attention should consult a qualified medical practitioner or suitable therapist. The directions for treatment of particular disorders and/or illnesses are given for the guidance of medical practitioners only, and should not be prescribed by those who do not have a medical training.

Temple Lodge Publishing Ltd.
Hillside House, The Square
Forest Row, RH18 5ES

www.templelodge.com

Published in English by Temple Lodge in 2021

Originally published in Dutch under the title *Je kunt er ook anders naar kijken Gedragsstoornissen bij kinderen en volwassenen met een verstandelijke beperking. Inzicht— begrip—behandeling* by Uitgeverij Christfoor, Zeist, in 2012

A CIP catalogue record for this book is available from the British Library

ISBN 978 1 912230 74 7

Cover by Morgan Creative
Typeset by Symbiosys Technologies, Visakhapatnam, India
Printed and bound by 4Edge Ltd., Essex

Contents

Introduction

It is with joy and hope that I present this book to the reader. Joy because I have managed to write down what I intended; hope that the reader will recognize my intention and be able to make use of the book for those who need it.

I myself have been impressed by the clarity of the six constitution types described in this book, and by the laws hidden within them. It might take a little while for the reader to recognize these laws, but they will not be hard to find if one always returns to the experience of these pictures within oneself (see exercises in Chapter 13). One will be able to understand each constitution type by repeatedly returning to the underlying causes, for instance 'a skin that is too thin' or 'a disturbed metabolism'. This will help one to begin to recognize aspects of the constitution types and to find a relationship to them.

The vision underpinning the theory of the constitution types originates in anthroposophy and is called 'the threefold nature of the human being'. This threefold approach describes three main functional areas in the human being, on the physical as well as on the psychological level. The three functional areas are interconnected. The threefold approach leads to a better understanding, while bringing coherence into the different aspects one may find within a human being. This will also enable us to relate certain types of behaviour to the underlying cause. Judgement and finding fault will be replaced by understanding, enabling us to penetrate more deeply into the core.

This book is about people with a learning disability and with behaviour that challenges services, and who are either being supported within the area of learning disabilities or in that of mental health. Most examples described in this book have been taken from these areas.

The data needed for diagnosing a constitution type is in some areas more comprehensive than in a mainstream diagnosis. The indications for support and approach that may then be given will therefore be more extensive and detailed in those particular areas, especially in relation to the life processes and to approach. The relationship with the overall picture will always remain visible on all levels. This will enable support workers and educators engaged in support and/or health care to com-municate with each other, leading to support plans and approaches that are fit for purpose and unified.

It is also possible to recognize regular syndromes like ADHD (Atten-tion Deficit and Hyperactive Disorder), ASD (Autism Spectrum Disor-der) and PDD-NOS (Pervasive Developmental Disorder, not otherwise specified) in the constitution types. Here, too, it might take some time to learn to see it, because, after all, this is all about 'looking at things differently'. This implies that by learning to see things differently one also develops oneself.

There are several ways of seeing or perceiving. Here I refer to a way of observing without judgement that allows communication within an unusual interpretive framework.

The book first describes an essential insight, namely that the core, or the individual 'I', of those with a mental health issue or a learning dis-ability is always healthy. Then the importance of recognizing healthy behaviour, in other words age-appropriate behaviour, will be discussed.

In Chapter 2 the term 'constitution type' will be explained so the reader will be able to follow the way of seeing and thinking used in this book, namely a method of looking without judging so as to enable communication within a different interpretive framework from usual.

This is followed by a short paragraph on the possible causes of clini-cal pictures in relation to the brain. This was done in order to place the contents of this book within the framework of contemporary scien-tific research. In this chapter I will also explain the ideas underpinning anthroposophic medicine. This type of medicine can be seen as comple-mentary to allopathic medication.

In Chapters 3 to 8 the six constitution types will be described. As many aspects as possible, from recognizing types of behaviour and the life processes to treatment and therapies, will be described through examples.

Using the method of 'observation through empathy' we will try and find out in Chapter 9 what it feels like to live with a particular consti-tution.

Chapter 10 deals with attachment disorders and traumas, because these problems often occur in people with learning disabilities and those presenting behavioural issues. Much has already been written about this subject and a number of additional aspects are described here.

Chapter 11 will show the relation of constitutional types with regular known disorders in different ways and comprises observation lists for use when assessing a constitution type.

Chapter 13 offers a number of exercises to help support workers develop their own skills to observe, recognize and experience what motivates a person with a particular constitution. It is the task of the caregiver/support worker to develop the creativity needed to come up with the right suggestions for a particular person in a particular situation. I have seen many wonderful examples of this.

Chapter 14 gives a good impression of the work with the constitution types on a 'care-farm' and in a therapeutic setting with examples from real-life situations.

Chapter 15, on the differences and similarities in the constitution types, may be helpful in assessing a constitution type. This chapter also offers an alternative way of forming a picture of the constitution types.

Acknowledgements

I remember the many people I met during the lessons, team meetings and workshops. By working together on this subject with enjoyment, we, or at least I, have learned much. The fruits of this work may be found in this book. I am especially grateful to Ursula Failenschmid for passing on her treasure trove of experience and knowledge, and I would like to thank Christie Amons for helping me find and bring order into the drawings and captions.

And last but not least, I would like to thank the children and adults who came to me looking for guidance and whom I have come to love so much.

1
Health and Healing

In his book *Education for Special Needs* Rudolf Steiner states: 'The "I" is always healthy.'[1]

Rudolf Steiner considers the awareness of this to be one of the most important conditions when supporting adults and children with a learning disability. The statement that the individual 'I' is healthy is a far-reaching one. The question remains why anyone would behave in a disturbed way against their own will? Hans Bom and Cor de Bode have a clear answer:

> The individual 'I' is characterized by a deep-seated universal will, the will to grow and become. Every parent knows that development is part of life. The idea that every human being has a unique individuality gives us deep trust in the meaning of the development of each human being. The individuality of a human being with a learning disability is just as perfect as that of any other person. The difference is that it is very hard for the individuality to show itself. The physical body, or in other words the 'house' of a person with a learning disability is not a suitable instrument for expressing the individuality.
>
> [...] The obstacles they meet in their 'instrument' belong to themselves and originate in a more deep-seated will that could be related to a former life. By overcoming or enduring these obstacles they will develop skills. Awareness of this may be very significant for the attitude of the support workers and educators of those with a learning difficulty.

It may raise a feeling of respect if the client is motivated to overcome obstacles. Support workers can also make contact out of their own individuality with the healthy individuality of the person they support or care for. The burdens and suffering may then be felt to be less hard. Experienced support workers will be intimately familiar with this phenomenon. Both the support worker and the person they support will be able to grow if they see the other one make progress in their development.[2]

It is often the case that a person will sense the development of their support worker. Here is an example:

Rob, a young man, who suffers from bouts of anxiety, comes into the day-care centre every day. He frequently displays compulsive behaviour. His parents bring him in the morning. Then he has to wait outside for ten minutes for the support workers to come.

A member of staff passes there every day and greets him. He will then cover his head with his hood and not respond. The staff member is struggling with problems in the team and is afraid that people are talking about him in a negative way. At home one evening he spends a good amount of time thinking about his anxiety and the problems with his colleagues. The next morning Rob greets him spontaneously and cheerfully.

The greatest gift for the person who is being supported is often when the support worker or educator begins to work on themselves.

Apart from the aspect of the healthy 'I' there is also the fact that every adult and child with a developmental impairment may display age-appropriate, and therefore healthy, behaviour, as well as behaviour that shows a delay in development. A person with a high IQ may have difficulties displaying healthy behaviour, either due to an accident, an illness or a hereditary problem.

Here is a quote from an autistic boy without speech who learned to write at the age of 16 without anyone knowing he had read and memorized many very complicated books. Here he describes how painful it is to realize that you do not fit within the social system.

> Indeed, I want you to know what it looks like on the inside in autistic children. Let's say that we are in a situation that cannot be compared with anything else. Can you imagine what it is like living in a social system that all of the time considers you to be 'mad'? Such a system cannot be right. I want everybody to know that autistic children are not stupid as is so often assumed. Without my writing I am not a real human being.[3]

By this statement, Birger Sellin shows how well he knows what he lacks and how deeply he longs to demonstrate his 'healthy' aspects. In many cases there is less of a difference between the IQ and the concrete abilities than in the case described here. Nevertheless it would help to diminish protest and miscommunication if a person of 15 or of 43 is addressed according to the responsibility appropriate to their age. It is not always possible, however, to demand age-appropriate skills. This point of view could be applied in relation to activities, games, work and learning materials on offer. The first example below is about lesson material, the second is about aggression.

> A class of 13 and 14-year-olds with moderate learning difficulties is listening with great interest to a simple physics lesson. Yet for most of them it would not be possible to reproduce or execute anything from this lesson. Some would be able to, but always only at their own level and in a different way.
>
> An adult who often displayed challenging behaviour towards objects and people, so that eventually he was no longer allowed to leave his room due to the risk, was addressed in the following way: 'We will do anything for you, so just tell us what you need. We will give you anything possible, but you have to stop hurting people and destroying things.' This was said repeatedly over a longer period of time and helped to establish better communication. Eventually his destructive behaviour disappeared too.[4]

In anthroposophic adult social care this principle is used in that all adult residents *have work* and are thus integrated into society as full citizens. Work as such has an inherent healing character.

Supporting people out of respect for their individuality demands an open and flexible attitude, free from norms and standards, and with knowledge of developmental psychology. Such an attitude leads to the kind of support that offers the children and adults challenges and opportunities within clear boundaries. For every child and adult with developmental difficulties a careful assessment must be made to establish which behavioural aspects belong to their particular phase of life—and are therefore healthy and demand a healthy challenge—and which ones do not.

Is a 'cure' possible?

Children need treatment in order to bring as much healing as possible to the area where there is delayed growth. This treatment may be pedagogical and educational, or medical or therapeutic, focusing on the life-functions.

Education is generally no longer appropriate in the field of adult social care. Yet it is essential to lessen the burden of suffering by way of medical or therapeutic support through the provision of a suitable environment[5] and the right approach.

The social approach, education, treatment, healing environment and therapies, as described in relation to the constitution types, have improved the quality of life of children and adults in many instances. Their skills have improved and they have learnt to manage their constitution more adequately, with or without help. Examples of this will be given in the case studies in Chapter 14. There will always be specific characteristics related to the constitution, as is the case with any other person. An actual cure to the level of 'normality' will usually only be possible if the disability is not serious.

Contemporary science: brain research into disorders

Brain research is conducted on a regular basis in people with disorders like ADHD (Attention Deficit and Hyperactive Disorder), epilepsy or the ASD (Autism Spectrum Disorder). Nowadays much research is also being done into causes of genetic and DNA disorders. With this type of research scientists regularly find causes that later appear not to be applicable to all people presenting the same clinical picture. This kind of research is still being conducted. In medical literature there are frequent reports that the cause of certain syndromes has not yet been discovered.

The anthroposophic approach to diagnostics includes brain function in its medical assessment, and additional questions are asked where there are irregularities: 'Why does the brain not function normally, what is causing this?' For instance, we can see that a brain scan shows up high wave fluctuations, as in epilepsy. This kind of brain scan gives certain indications. The next question would be: 'Why does the scan show such high wave fluctuations?' Could there be a different physical cause for this? We do then actually find a cause for this brain condition. This cause would also explain the behavioural phenomena of this clinical picture (see Chapter 5, 'congested constitution').

This would also apply to the diagnosis of ADHD. It is said that there is a lack of synapses in the brain. A physical cause has in the last few years been found for the brain condition in people with ADHD namely in the inability to digest definite products (see Chapter 8, 'the "too light" constitution'). These questions originate from exact observation of disorders on several levels (see Chapter 12, 'Diagnostic Methodology').

By means of regular scientific methods it is not always possible to find proof for the answers obtained on the basis of anthroposophic diagnostics. Nevertheless developments in scientific approach are providing increasingly more answers than was possible at the time (1923) when these constitution types were first described. There are often similarities to Steiner's statements, but contemporary scientific methods also leave many questions unanswered.

Below is a contribution from an anthroposophic physician who spent a long time researching children with a delayed development:

> The entire human organism is the instrument not just for the central nervous system, but also for the spirit and the soul. The actual problematic area is usually situated in the metabolic system and its organs, where the will is supported. Already in 1921 in a course for physicians Steiner gave the advice to find the knowledge of mental illness in the direction of the excretions, as they give ultimate insight into the metabolic processes.[6]

Apart from the anthroposophic supportive methods, all kinds of complementary treatments have been developed, including methods that have a direct effect on the physical body. Examples of these are elimination diets and ketogenic diets used in the treatment of ADHD and epilepsy.

Medication

Psychotropic drugs and anthroposophic medication

For certain disorders in adults and children with a developmental impairment psychotropic drugs can be helpful in slowing down or stimulating the symptoms of activity or passivity in the brain. In most cases drugs will target the symptoms.

The question remains as to the actual cause of the disturbance in the brain. A well-known example is depression. In depression there seems to be a reduction in the amount of the substance serotonin. The production of serotonin is then stimulated via medication. The actual physiological cause of depression is not known, but there are a number of known factors that may trigger or exacerbate depression.

In the period during which such medication is being used, space and quiet is created in which new behaviour may be learned through education, therapy or other means. The long-term effects of certain medications that are being prescribed are not known. So there is the possibility that the actual remedy is not the substance that is being given but rather the acquisition of new behaviour.

Anthroposophic medication is aimed at providing a model for the body and not just for the brain. If a particular organ in the body proves to be weak, a medicine is prescribed that 'demonstrates' the healthy condition of this organ.

> Anthroposophic medicine has its place whenever it is possible to direct or enhance the self-regulating functioning of the organism.[7]

The human body comprises the four elements of water, earth, air and fire or warmth. Plants, minerals and animals also comprise these elements. The elements found in the human body in certain combinations must therefore also be present in nature. Thorough research has shown that there are substances from plants, minerals and animals that may have a healing effect on certain organs and organic areas in the form of a medicine.

Take bryophyllum, for example. This plant's characteristic of protecting itself by means of a wax coating on its stem and leaves is of special importance for the medicine. Part of this plant, diluted many times, is administered as a medicine known as Bryophyllum for emotional anxiety and stress.

Another example is the product known as Conchae which is in part made of shells. As a medicine it provides protection against external influences in the way a shell does.

Likewise, medicines have been developed that, also in cases of behavioural problems, can provide support and/or healing on the path towards more harmony.

2
Constitution and Constitution Types

Everybody has a constitution. Your constitution is the interaction between physical, biological, behavioural and individual aspects. All these aspects are interconnected and function as a whole, which is called a constitution. Everyone's constitution is different.

A person's constitution is present in rudimentary form before birth and is determined by hereditary, individual and environmental factors. The hereditary factors play a major role in the shaping of a human being, although they are not necessarily fixed for the whole of life. Hereditary factors can be transformed by environmental influences, illness or self-education. The individual aspects as part of the constitution are the inherent, unique aspects of this particular human being.

From an anthroposophic point of view, the individual 'I' of a human being is always sound. The individual aspect cannot be perceived physically which is exactly why it can remain sound. The individual 'I' uses the body as an instrument. A brilliant violinist may perform a beautiful concert while using an excellent violin, but if there is something wrong with the violin this would put the player at a disadvantage.

The division into six constitution types is related to the three main functional areas, (see below) in the human body and in human behaviour. In the human body they are: the neuro-sensory system, the rhythmic system and the system of metabolism and limbs. In human behaviour we can distinguish thinking, feeling and will.

With a sound development these three areas form a more or less coherent unit. If the development was disturbed, one or more aspects have become too one-sided, stuck or poorly integrated.

It is self-evident that when speaking about constitution types we refer to large groupings of people. Within these groupings various different aspects of movement, posture, behaviour and outer appearance will be similar, and these then will form a whole picture. When observing each individual human being we will always take into account personal aspects as well as their constitution.

The three main functional areas in the human being are so all-encompassing that all symptoms may be included within them. The three functional areas and the constitution types have been described below.

TIGHT				LOOSE
Closed				**Open**
one-sidedness	behaviour	physical	behaviour	one-sidedness
compulsive	thinking	neuro-sensory system	thinking	forgetful
congested	feeling	rhythmic system	feeling	open
heavy	will	metabolic-limb system	willing	light

The six constitution types are based on the life processes. These happen on a deeper, subconscious level and cannot be changed easily, although they greatly influence behaviour and well-being.

The threefold model outlined above indicates where the disturbance may be seen most clearly, namely in the neuro-sensory system in the area of thinking, in the rhythmic system in the feeling and in the metabolic-limb system in the area of movement.

In the 'too light' constitution type, for instance, the one-sidedness will be expressed in movement as a result of organic problems. As such the other two areas, those of feeling and of thinking, are not really out of balance, but their balance may be disturbed due to the urge to move, yet, as soon as the person is in a space of complete quiet their thinking appears to function better and social abilities appear to be present.

The concept of the threefold human nature clarifies this principle in such a way that it may also be applied to the other constitutions.

Life processes cannot be changed easily:

> As to temperament, character and inclinations the human being changes much more slowly than in the realm of mental pictures and thoughts. A hot-headed child will only change very slowly. Temperament, character and inclinations often persist all through life. Ideas and experiences change quickly; it is just the opposite with temperament,

character and inclinations. They are very tenacious; they change like the hour-hand of a clock compared to the minute-hand. This is because these things take place in the etheric body, which only changes very slowly, much more slowly than the astral body. [8]

This slow change is reflected in the sometimes trivial daily habits you encounter in yourself and in others, for instance in where you want certain things to be, the way you do the cleaning, where you put your keys etc. This view of the constitution types may give an important contribution at this level.

> During a workshop an elderly couple began to quarrel there and then about how to position the toilet roll: with the loose end to the front or to the back. This quarrel had been going on ever since they had moved in together.

Here is a brief description of the six constitution types in healthy people:

1. *Compulsive*. Good in thinking, remembering, categorizing. Less good in feeling, expressing emotions, sympathizing. Somewhat slow in taking action.
2. *Forgetful*. Enthusiastic, imaginative, less profound. Difficulties remembering. Slow development, not good at learning. Social, the life and soul of the party.
3. *Congested*. Deeply hidden thoughts, little empathy. Sombre. Does not easily act for other people, is solitary. Strong-willed, persevering.
4. *Open*. Very sensitive, deep empathy with others. Likes to care for those who are weaker. Aesthetic, artistic. Is alert and has much to digest. Critical.
5. *Heavy*. Good-natured, helpful. Keeps going for a long time, once started. Slow to start, slow to react, good observer.
6. *Light*. Very active, quick to organize things. Gets things done first and thinks afterwards. Likes to do things for others, is socially skilful, yet superficial.

Some preliminary remarks to the chapters on the constitution types

In the following chapters a mixture of knowledge from anthroposophic and mainstream sources has been used.

In this chapter the constitution types have been described in pairs recognizable as opposites (polarities) underpinned by causes situated within the same area of the body.

If you wish to find out whether a particular constitution type fits to a child or adult it might be helpful to turn to the chapter on diagnostics after having read about the six types.

Many symptoms may be found in any of the six types but always in a different way. Obsessions and challenging behaviour, for instance, may be found in each of the constitution types, so there will also be six different ways to treat and approach them (see Chapter 15).

Practice has shown that it is almost always possible to link someone to one of the constitution types. Sometimes it is possible to recognize symptoms from several types. This could have two possible reasons:

- One has overlooked the fact that many different kinds of behaviour are possible in each of the types. Anyone can become angry without it being pathological. This is about *behaviour that is too one-sided* which is what the characteristics in the following chapters are based on.
- Behaviour has been the main consideration and this may vary depending on the environment. The life processes remain more stable.

3
Constitution Type 1—Too Compulsive

An example

Sylvia is a very independent woman, age 33 (in Mental Health Care, verbal IQ 80, OCD [Obsessive Compulsive Disorder]), with small stature, dark hair and dark brown eyes. Her cheeks are red and nicely rounded and the chin protrudes. She always walks as if in a hurry, with a searching look. She does not see the people she meets, apart from those she knows well. Then she will rush towards them to talk about one of her favourite topics: football scores. She talks fast, often looking away and usually not listening to the reply.

In her leisure time she likes to solve crossword puzzles and then send them in, or she will play a game by herself so she will always win. She knows exactly where on the premises of the institution she will be able to get hold of the newspaper with the football scores most easily and if there is none, she will know where to find another copy, as she simply *has* to have it! If necessary, she will burst into every room until she has found one.

Sylvia has another typical trait: although she is quite able and independent, she never uses the telephone, not even to talk to her parents.

Outer Appearance

People who show these characteristics are often somewhat stocky with a sturdy build, although sometimes they may be slender. They usually have dark hair and dark eyes (see 'Interpretation'). Also fair-haired people with blue eyes may show compulsions but for reasons unrelated to the constitution.

Their physical and facial features are usually beautiful and well-formed and the appearance is harmonious and shapely. The hair-do and clothing are usually neat and elegant.

Posture, movement, motor skills

Posture

The posture is not supple or agile. They are often standing with hunched shoulders and you can see tension in neck, shoulders and torso. They make a downcast impression. Sometimes this is only slightly perceptible and sometimes it is really obvious. Eye contact is rare, yet people with these characteristics will look around alertly and intently. Sometimes they seem to look right through you. Their gaze is tense and serious, rarely light and sparkling. They have few facial expressions and you cannot tell much from their face.

Movement

The movements may seem wooden and clumsy, for instance in running: the legs remain stiff and in the same stance; they tend to land heavily and will not bounce back up easily; the upper body as well as the arms remain rigidly in the same position. The movements are not well coordinated or supple, which gives an impression of old age. People with these traits will join in with games, sports and gymnastics, but in a clumsy way. They do not manage the more difficult exercises in sports and gymnastics.

> Matthew age 14, in care, (TIQ [Total Intelligence Quota] 70, ASD) has been given nice roller-blades. He proudly puts them on and goes outside. There we see him strutting about on his roller-blades, lifting his legs up high with every step.

People who show these characteristics often also find swimming difficult and prefer not to lift their feet off the ground. They often prefer to stay inside, unless they have an obsession related to nature. They will frequently repeat and be unable to stop particular movements, such as sweeping, sawing, washing the dishes, cleaning a spot on the car, opening and closing the door or tapping. They will react to physical contact by becoming rigid and they find it hard to relax and move towards others. They don't perceive physical contact as pleasant, making them appear somewhat unapproachable.

Motor skills

Also the fine motor skills are often clumsy and tense. Some people who show these traits, however, are good at crafts and needlework, but one can always see from their work that they were doing it with too much tension or force. If they are good at making a particular thing or if it is related to an obsession, they will want to make it again and again until their room is filled with it.

Life processes

The hands and feet tend to be cold and dry to the touch and also the skin feels dry and closed off. People showing these characteristics are often choosy with food and will arrange each component separately on their plate, picking at it like a mouse, while pushing aside what they do not like. They usually only like what they are familiar with. Others rather tend to eat greedily and quickly without chewing or breaks. They tend to have trouble with constipation, causing abdominal strain and making them feel unwell. Some tend to drink a lot.

The breathing can be shallow and they are unable to breathe out properly. People who show these traits usually remain small in stature for a long time, suddenly growing fast during puberty and will often have acne and excessive perspiration.

Their sexual development is usually very slow and limited. In late puberty excessive masturbation often occurs. They have a poor body image. Often they do not feel any pain, tiredness or cold, nor will they notice when they are ill. With their acute sense of orientation some people who show these characteristics appear to be able to make very precise observations that are more profound than usual.

> Karsten (age 13, learning disabilities, TIQ 40, ASD, speaks a few words) is taken by car from Amsterdam to a place in the vicinity of Utrecht. As soon as he arrives, he runs inside looking for crayons and a large sheet of paper and draws the exact map of the route they have travelled.

All those showing these traits to a certain degree have problems with being touched, and they are easily startled because they hardly experience their body. Being touched only on the shoulders or receiving a massage is easier for them. If they have a fever once in a while, the wooden, introverted and anxious behaviour may well disappear and they can be warm and open.

They thoroughly dislike being touched by water, both when being washed, but also when swimming and playing with water. If they can dress themselves they take care of their clothes meticulously.

Behaviour

Thinking and perceiving

In infancy people who display the characteristics of the 'too compulsive' constitution are often very alert. They lie wide-eyed, quietly observing the environment while nothing escapes their attention. The emphasis is on the perception, not on moving or dozing. Sometimes they will object to touch already at an early age. They are often diagnosed with ASD.

If they learn to speak—which is not always the case—they will pronounce the words very exactly and with emphasis. You will not hear much tonal differentiation in the words and there is hardly any melody in a sentence. Speaking sounds mechanical, monotonous and abrupt and sometimes also a little slow and stuttering.

They will ask many 'why'-questions. They want to know all the ins and outs and will not stop asking. They hear the reply, but seem not to take it 'in'. The reply never seems to satisfy them, apart from for a moment if it is the one they expected. The connections between things remain largely invisible to them.

In her book, *Autism, A very short introduction,* Uta Frith wrote about the ability of people with ASD to distinguish shapes, while the meaning is less important to them. They may, for instance, do a jigsaw puzzle upside down. She attributes this to poor central coherence. In some cases, on the other hand, it may be extra good.

Certain fragments from a sentence, topics or events tend to keep coming back to them. They are unable to forget or process them and will repeat them over and over again. The reason for this could be an experience that made a deep impression on them or was shocking, but it is not always possible to trace it back. Sometimes attention remains focused on one and the same subject, often a technical one, such as the elevator, the self-closing door, the washing machine, lights or a mobile phone. They will talk exclusively about this subject, make drawings of it and try and find it.

Neil (age 44, in Learning Disability Care, TIQ 50, ASD) always walks around or into houses or buildings with a tense, searching look on his face. He is short and slight, yet wiry. Whenever he sees a door with a door-closer he cannot be stopped, will run to it and open it. While flapping his arms and jumping lightly up and down he keeps looking how the door closes again very slowly as if driven by an invisible power. Meanwhile, Neil does not hear or see anything else. As soon as the door has shut, he will run back to it to open it again. If it was up to him, he would do this all day long. He knows exactly which shops in the village have doors with a door-closer and refuses to go to any other shops.

Others may have several favourite subjects although the same questions and themes will return again and again. They are unable to forget, digest or process these things. They are captured in a cycle of always the same thoughts and images and are full of them. There is no room for anything new. You will see an urge to make 'contact' so they can get rid of what is stuck in their head. They may become famous for their mastery of numbers, their ability to tell on what day of the week someone was born once they know the birthdate, to know bus and train timetables by heart or to operate a computer faultlessly.

Feeling

People with compulsions are anxious. In many this manifests in the stereotypical phantasies of the pictures they draw. The threat of destruction by monsters, dragons and explosions are recurrent items. They also tend to draw schematic people, trees and houses with thick outlines and/or fully coloured in. In their pictures they will draw every single detail in the way they must have actually seen it as if in a photograph, for instance every roof tile is drawn with a sharp pencil and precisely the way it 'should' look.

People with these characteristics feel supported by certain actions, structures, spatial planning and rituals. If these fall away or have been changed without the person having been carefully prepared in advance, anxiety or a panic attack will come about followed by aggression. They will scream, self-harm or smash up things around them. Such a reaction can be very coercive for those around them. Some tyrannize their family with their fearful outbursts and scenes to such a degree that in the end family life is all about the performing of certain rituals: if this is not done properly, one has to start all over again. Everybody becomes infected by this fear.

I read an article on the internet that exactly describes the contents of this chapter:

> This type of person has a very restricted emotional life; you will rarely or never see them truly sad or laugh heartily. You will not see them enjoy

something sweet or something beautiful. They do not talk about their feelings, apart from occasionally about their panic or a physical sensation arising from it (and then only for a very short time). They have low self-esteem and a lot of self-criticism, often as if coming from an 'inner voice' that expresses negative criticism and shame. They have a sense of having lost control of their own impulses, are inclined to touch, count and feel things far beyond reason. They tend to feel that their thoughts are directed by others and that they are unable to stop them.[9]

Although there is a real longing for it, there is not usually any inner urge to make contact with others, because their head is full of images. The 'Son-Rise' programme is a response to this. The behaviour of a person with ASD is imitated so they recognize it and contact may come about. This may lead to an expansion of activities and abilities. They often do not take in other people's annoyance, anger or grief.

You will not see them daydreaming or imagining things freely. Their imagination is not creative, but predictable and stereotypical and sometimes almost absurd. Some have clear, fixed ideas about their future.

> Reuben (age 7, in Learning Disability Care, TIQ 50, ASD) has very dark skin. He does not speak. When Black Peter [in the Dutch tradition he is St Nicholas's black servant, tr.] comes into the classroom, he is the only one to get up, not at all impressed. He comes forward, wets a finger and brushes away a little of the black from Black Peter's cheek. Then he calmly ambles back to his seat.

People with these characteristics are often socially not really compliant or flexible. They will either isolate themselves from others or decide how things should be done. They easily get into a panic when others move or act in unexpected ways. This may then soon set off a quarrel causing other people or children to withdraw. They do not have the ability to imagine what other people feel. They are caught up in mental pictures and certain actions. This makes them appear aloof, wretched and a little sad, as if they are behind a glass wall and are unable to find the way through to warm contact.

This can make those around them feel powerless. Not being able to make real contact with them is difficult to accept and to bear.

> Chris (age 48, in Mental Health Care, TIQ 80, OCD) is very self-centred and has a traumatic background. He is especially interested in

people who have been in trouble with a support worker. Whenever the conversation is about sex, violence or death, a grin will appear on his face and he will echo one's words and be unable to stop talking about it. No one manages to stop him. Chris also tends to touch people and might even take someone by the throat if the conversation is about strangulation or 'water-boarding'.

Doing

Adults and children with these traits long for sameness, uniformity and perfection. They would like things to proceed as they always have and will establish clear patterns in their daily life. The things in their room have fixed places, they dress according to a fixed pattern and the bed is made without a crease in the bedcover. They will immediately notice if something has been put in a different place and will hurry to 'correct' it: it just *has* to be done! It is not advisable to stop them from doing this or to try to divert them, as this may only succeed with those who only have a mild form of the compulsive disorder.

Because they are so observant they have a good overview and can be very helpful with small tasks, which they will do meticulously. They are good at explaining things they know well and will tell you exactly how things should be done and where to find things.

> John (age 12, in Mental Health Care, TIQ 70, MCDD [Multiple Complex Developmental Disorder]) just has to get up every time someone passes by the window, which has half-curtains. He cannot be stopped from doing this and, should anyone try, he will panic. Only after some time it was understood that John tried to find out if the invisible part of the people passing by was actually attached to them. You can often see him outside, pacing up and down the pavement and self-absorbed.
>
> He likes playing 'buses' of which he knows the timetable by heart, or you might hear him with an agitated voice like a sports-commentator covering a football match.

Children and adults with these characteristics are good at taking on certain projects if they want to make something. They have an exact picture of how it should look. If in the process problems occur you will have to help them, otherwise they will destroy their work out of sheer frustration. It may be that they do not even want to work on it any longer, as it would anyway go wrong. 'I am sure I will fail again' or 'I don't want to do it'. They detest soiling their hands or their clothing with clay, glue etc. They will also become anxious when presented with a large white sheet of paper which they have to fill with crayon or paint. Their perfectionism then becomes an obstacle for them and there is no way to divert them from this. If they are well supported, however, their perfectionism and excellent ability to observe may lead to the most beautiful results: one young man used to make splendid ceramic tea sets, and a woman with compulsive behaviour was very good at engraving glass.

> Martin (age 28, Mental Health Care, TIQ 90, ASD) had been living in an institution for a long time. Now he lives independently and has a support worker who looks in on him every now and then. He has a permanent job as an archivist. He is doing well and he likes the job, although he appears a little tense. At weekends he is always occupied with music. He plays the guitar and has friends with the same taste in music.

Once such a possibility has been found they will persevere and work long and hard until they have learnt or fully completed something, if they have been given the space to do so.

Interpretation

Most people with these traits are diagnosed with ASD or OCD (which are classed as anxiety disorders). This occurs more frequently in child-hood and more in boys than in girls.

Those with compulsions are unable to forget. Ideas and thoughts do not sink down. Certain ideas need to be converted into actions or be spoken out loud.

In order to be able to let go of impressions and thoughts it is necessary to be a little less awake for a moment and to learn to be more objective, after which one will be able to focus one's attention on something else. In this state of learning to be more objective and becoming somewhat dreamy one can reach one's feelings and give them a place, as long as one finds some inner peace. As soon as an impression has been let go of, it will sink down, enabling one to forget it. If there is an inability to digest it emotionally (shock, trauma), it will keep recurring and will sometimes keep one awake at night.

A person with compulsions has a limited ability to let go, find inner peace and become dreamy. The area of feeling is poorly developed and the person is much too awake. Impressions cannot be properly processed and digested and getting into action is hard. Their learning disability may be an additional obstacle, especially in relation to developing an overview and perspective.

As soon as an impression is forgotten it will become a memory, which can be recalled. From an anthroposophic point of view, memories are stored on the surface of the organs.

Ideas, impressions and images are stored as the essence of the original observations. People who do not have a compulsive constitution but have partially digested traumatic memories may also suffer from cramps and illnesses such as stomach ulcers, stomach cramps and heart problems, and later on also from nightmares.

In the book, *Education for Special Needs, the Curative Education Course* by Rudolf Steiner we can read that obsessions are mental pictures that all the time bounce back against the surface of the organs. The surface of the organs (and maybe of all cells), where the memories should have been stored, does not absorb them, either because it is too hard and/ or too cold or too tense, like an inflated ball that you can push in a little, but that will bounce back immediately. Haptonomy★ therapists work with the phenomenon that memories are 'stored' somewhere in the body. Also experiences by people after an organ transplant show a connection between memories and the organs. They notice that they begin to do things they did not do before and that these belonged to the deceased owner of the organ.[10]

So far, little is known in mainstream science about the origin of compulsions. Too much iron in proportion to sulphur will cause premature hardening of the organs and a darkish skin, dark eyes and dark hair. The proportion of sulphur to iron demands a certain balance (see also the 'too forgetful' constitution type). If people have a naturally dark skin it would be better to concentrate on the behavioural aspects.

> A poorly developed metabolic and limbs system may cause a low level of sulphur in the protein ....The [chemical parameters] are not the usual ones. Then it happens that compulsive ideas begin to show themselves in the person's organism...[11]

★ the science of affectivity, tr.

Causes

- An iron-rich constitution.
- Traumatic experiences in the first seven years while the organs are still being formed, or hardening through tensing up (trauma). This can also occur if there is no iron-rich constitution.
- Demands put on intellectual capacities too early.
- A strongly authoritarian, tyrannical upbringing (the person experiences profound anxieties and becomes tense).
- This disorder may be hereditary.[12]

In some cases the compulsive disorder will only begin to show in puberty. This happens to open, sensitive people who easily tend to get anxious and have tensed up inwardly over a long period of time as a consequence of their sensitivity (open constitution). Some may develop a psychosis in puberty, because the young person is unable to deal with their emotions becoming more powerful during that time of life. They may then lose an overview and be overcome by anxiety.[13]

Supportive approach

Motto: warmth and movement, relaxation and promoting a dreamy state.
Deeper anxiety: rigidity.
Greatest desire: relaxation.

The most important thing in the supportive approach to people with these characteristics is, as much as possible, to subdue and lessen the inclination to become too alert and hardened, and to stimulate physical activity.

It is essential that support workers or teachers are not drawn into the anxiety behind the compulsions, because they would then equally get caught up in them and be unable to adequately support the person any longer. Always avoid saying 'no', 'none', 'never', 'not'. Coercing, confronting or prohibiting are of no use. It would be better to gently teach people to take very good care of themselves in a peaceful state.

Many of the following indications for support may also be found in literature about ASD, especially the indications about structure and predictability.

In the life sphere

In whatever is done to help a person in such a situation, care should be taken not to increase their alertness. This means approaching them slowly and gently in the morning, and always doing things in the same way, quietly and with peaceful gestures. A slow and somewhat dreamy way of speaking will encourage them to do the same. Any sudden action will increase their alertness.

It is good to give a preview of the day and illustrate this with picture-cards or let them tell about it themselves. Emphasizing what has changed will help prepare them for it. For some, even a change of spread on the breakfast table may be a reason for a mighty temper tantrum. Once one has got to know them one will recognize the signs or become alert to what is too hard for them to cope with.

Clothing and nutrition, etc.

Warmth is very helpful, not only in clothing (coats, hats and scarves), when getting washed, and in room temperature, but also in food and environment.

It is good to pay special attention to decreasing iron-rich foods and increasing sulphur-rich foods. Iron has a hardening effect, while sulphur softens, enhancing absorption. A detailed list of sulphur-rich and iron-rich foods may be found at the end of the next chapter.

It is interesting to note that sulphur-rich foods especially comprise fruit, flowers etc. These are food products that have been ripened by much warmth from the sun.

Also skin oils may be used to increase warmth, at first only on the shoulders and the neck. In the morning or in the evening, a massage may be given with a warming or relaxing oil. This should be done very carefully and in peace and, where appropriate, as prescribed by a physician. Some people will not be able to bear this kind of touch. A warm bath with lavender bath milk may work miracles.

A cup of good lavender tea given in the evening may help decrease wakefulness. A camomile compress or simply a hot-water bottle on the stomach could also help the person grow pleasantly drowsy and fall asleep. It is important to provide an environment that is well-organized with an occasional change. Warm colours like salmon pink, light violet, very soft light green and natural materials can have a positive effect.

Independence and approach

Most people who show these characteristics are quite independent in daily life as long as there is a fixed routine. Sometimes it may be necessary to help them get going, gently and, above all, with a great deal of humour. Very simple humour has a liberating effect, and laughing can relieve tensions. As they are so alert, they will often be able to grasp a literal joke, for instance when you imitate their behaviour. They need help to learn social skills that others take for granted.

A good way of helping people let go of their fixations is by working with images: describing the present situation in an image and thus bringing movement into it. This could simply be the image of a stubborn donkey, a train that is starting up or an inquisitive professor who suddenly wants something nice to eat and therefore rushes off to his delicious breakfast.

The obsession may be exaggerated a bit by small deliberate actions so you can laugh about it together. For instance you could make the jar of peanut butter, that for them always has to be on the table, disappear for a moment and then together make it magically reappear. The art is to always think of something new.

> A woman who would often bang her head against a wall was told very quietly: 'The wall should not bang your head.' Then suddenly she looked at the wall in amazement and the habit stopped for a while. If said too often it would no longer work.

They love it when you enter into their world once in a while. It will make contact easier. The 'Son-Rise method', also known as the 'Kaufman method' is based on this principle.

It is essential to teach young people and adults self-knowledge as a basis for them to take certain measures in an ever more independent way.

It will always be necessary to bring small changes into fixed patterns but only after having discussed them with the person in question (or having made them visible through a check-list). Fixation alone will obviously not be effective, but help can only come through flexibility.

If the person gets stuck in a routine or an action one might be able to 'whisper' it away. For instance, someone might want to hear your watch tick every half a minute. Then you could say softly: 'Forget the watch…leave the watch…, you are doing fine…, let it go…' You keep repeating this every now and then, evermore quietly. It will be most effective, if you yourself become dreamy too.

It might also be necessary to curb the obsession in order to prevent those around the person constantly having to suffer from it and becoming annoyed and negative. Then, in a positive way, an arrangement is made with the person, that particular words or persistent questions/ actions are only allowed at a certain place or time and otherwise not. This is a behavioural therapy technique that is in itself not specifically healing, but will make living with the person more bearable.

The arrangements that have been made must be carried out consistently, clearly and with neutrality and understanding.

Activities, play and work
Learning to feel, experience, enjoy and then act instead of thinking is an important part of the approach.

— With young children this can be developed by often speaking in a kind of sing-song way and by stimulating play and imagination in various ways. It would, for instance, be better to let them work with thick crayons or paint brushes rather than with a pen or a black pencil, so as to prevent hardened images.
— As much as possible try to involve the child or adult in games, activities, dance and sports, also together with others, for instance by giving the person special tasks or jobs they could fulfil.
— Let them listen to a story or music in dimmed light. Listening will make them dreamy and they will enjoy it more. Let them get used to being touched.
— Painting, singing and making music can enhance the emotional life and experience of young people and adults. This will also help them to practise listening and observing out of interest, which is completely different from doing it because of an obsession. Drama may be a possibility if they can be motivated to do it.
— Care should be taken that children and adults with these characteristics are in movement in any way possible (work). It is also important that they work with their hands as much as they can, making things they can be proud of!
— In general, it is important not to stimulate them with too many impressions and information. This means that for those with this particular

constitution TV, movies, computer games and loud music are not recommended. Obsessions may then again increase very quickly.

— Learning to distinguish between different emotions and to recognize them, first in themselves and later on in others. Developing a gentle attitude towards themselves.

— In young people and adults mirroring the obsession can be helpful, for instance by imitation or exaggeration without making fun of them (exposure therapy). The purpose of this is to show them what they are doing and allow them to laugh about it, thus enabling them to let go of the obsession. Sometimes, with adults, one could call up a counter-picture to the obsession, thus avoiding the need to imitate it: for instance washing your hands in dirty water. You will notice that the anxiety will disappear if you keep it up long enough.

Peter (age 10, in Learning Disability Care, TIQ 60, ASD), who has an obsession with lamps, could be very happy for a while while drawing and constructing cardboard houses with lamps in them. He would invent ever more variations. Now that he is a bit older he is allowed to help the electrician, which he loves. It also keeps him moving which is helping him.

Forbidding or preventing a compulsion does not make any sense. It only increases the tension and therefore also the anxiety, leading to more and new compulsions or fixations emerging. For adults, cognitive behavioural therapy could be helpful. Those who are helped to let go of their obsessions are unbelievably grateful to their support workers. Their need for contact is just as great as anyone else's, but they lack the ability to show it. A compulsion is like a prison, and the feeling that they are doing things wrong all the time appears to be always present.

Supportive measures

— Medication

As for (anthroposophic) medication, sulphur may be given (also in the diet) to improve the proportion of sulphur to iron. Medication may be given that has a warming and dissolving effect on the metabolism, as well as medication that strengthens the emotional life and evokes a dreamy state of mind. A medicine commonly used is Argentum, a sulphuric compound with metals.

— External physical measures
Incarnating, calming, warming oil applications ('Einreibungen'), massage or compresses can be used in many different ways. Also baths can have the effect of warming, bringing flow, loosening and relaxation (see also the section on 'clothing and nutrition'.) Sulphur baths, liver therapy.

— Physiotherapy
Swimming and frequent and intensive use of the limbs in general.

— Eurythmy therapy
Moving to the sound of vowels, among other things, can open up and bring flow, also in the breathing. Make rigid movements more flexible.

— Healing environment
Order and tidiness with an occasional change. Everything has a clear function. Warm, dreamy colours.

— Art therapy
On the one hand trying to soften the surplus of form by adding colour or water or by making a concrete form more abstract. On the other hand teaching them to look more closely: although awake they will often not see things as they really are. Let them paint or model things that are in a process of metamorphosis: caterpillar—chrysalis—butterfly, seed—plant—flower—fruit—seed.
　　Changing a colour by mixing it.
　　Dynamic drawing.
　　Modelling: working with solid earth.

— Music therapy
The pure, objective quality of music can be a blessing for them. Music has a wonderful, mathematical order. In the therapy they are allowed to become dreamy, experience emotions and come into movement through rhythm or dance. Songs and tone-sequences may be chosen that have a liberating and expansive effect. Letting them sing or play themselves can be very helpful.

— Drama therapy
In drama therapy one can work with concrete life-situations in which there is anxiety or a feeling of isolation. These situations may be acted

out in order to see what further actions this person can take. The person's imagination can be stimulated.

— Play therapy

Play therapy gives an opportunity to give concrete form to threatening fears and, with the help of the therapist, transforming them or loosening up fixed patterns. They can learn to deal with compulsions and to gain social skills.

— Anthroposophic therapeutic speech and regular speech therapy

In therapeutic speech it is helpful to work with open vowels, words and sentences that change, or with humour. Speaking with modulation (instead of monotonously) and deepening the breathing may have a healing effect.

— Cognitive Behavioural Therapy (CBT)

This may be very helpful for young people and adults with an IQ above 50 and over 10 years of age. They can be helped with learning to control their thoughts, explore their feelings and experience connections.

— Family therapy and family support

These are important for understanding and accepting the situation. All family members can be made aware of what it feels like to be ruled by fear and they can practise consistent behaviour step by step.

4
Constitution Type 2—Too Forgetful

An example

Susan (age 9, in Learning Disability Care, TIQ 40, ASD) has fair hair, red cheeks and an open expression. She is always enthusiastic about all kinds of plans, is easy-going and pleasant to be with.

And yet she seems insecure. She often asks the same questions and, for her age, she does not dare to undertake much by herself. She is willing to do what is asked of her and she is helpful with the younger children, but if you leave her alone nothing really happens or she will continue to do what she thinks you would like her to do. Sometimes unexpected things happen: excrement is found in children's coat pockets and food that has gone bad between the clothes in a wardrobe. This can only have been Susan.

Outer appearance

Characteristics of this constitution are: fair, reddish or red hair; pale, dry and sensitive skin (sometimes with freckles), cold, dry hands (as opposed to those with a 'too open' constitution); roundish, childlike, fine features of the face and the body; light-blue to grey-green eyes. Usually the figure is full, but not fat.

We have learned from experience that there are also people with this constitution who do not have fair or red hair, but do have many of the other characteristics. It seems too restrictive to determine a certain constitution by the colour of the hair, as this constitution also occurs in people with dark skin and hair.

Posture, movement, motor skills

Posture
The upper body is usually bent slightly forwards and the shoulders are pulled up a little, giving the posture a somewhat 'hunched' impression.

The facial features can be lively and interested but often passive. The eyes then tend to stare or look into the distance. Children and adults with these characteristics also often have an anxious or insecure look in their eyes. Also in their movements and posture they appear more childlike than one would expect for their age. They like to walk next to someone, sometimes holding on to their arm.

Movement

The movement patterns of people with characteristics of the 'too forgetful' constitution may vary strongly. Sometimes they are excited, restless and will flit here and there. At other times you can see them sitting still, seemingly plunged into a void, often with their mouth slightly open.

They might suddenly start to run and then stop or change direction unexpectedly.

Their movements are often supple and light. People with a more severely delayed development may have typical movement patterns like rocking, stamping of feet, jumping, hitting the thighs with the fists or banging the head on the table.

Motor skills

The spontaneous movements of people showing traits of being 'too forgetful' can be supple and agile. They tend to be impulsive and wild, but as soon as they have to do something consciously it becomes more difficult. Learning to walk, cycle, climb and swim is not easy for them. Their fine motor skills tend to be late for their age and clumsy (dyspraxia). They may write in a messy way and have problems with handwork, also because of their forgetfulness. A latent anger (stress) may also affect their fine motor skills.

They will join in with sports a little absent-mindedly and are not really bothered about achievements or winning, or simply want to win in spite of having forgotten the rules. In their dreamy state they are often afraid of the ball. They move to music gracefully, but conscious steps in folk dancing are hard, if not impossible.

Life processes

As has been mentioned earlier, the skin is dry, often rough and sometimes there is a tendency to develop eczema. The warmth is unequally distributed over the body: some areas are cold, others warm and some are red and blotchy.

Sometimes calloused skin may be found on the outside of the hands due to frequent biting or knocking.

The breathing is usually shallow. The appetite is good and there is a tendency to eat quickly. It is interesting that some people tend to choose foods that are good for them, like iron-rich food, (see diet list for iron/sulphur-rich at the end of this chapter) while others do exactly the opposite. Some tend to play with their food.

There might be a particular, baby-like odour. Sweaty feet occur frequently but the perspiration does not have a pungent smell.

> Rianne (age 34, learning disability, V(erbal)IQ of 20, ASD) loves to take a full bath with as much foam as possible. She adores the foam, will take it in her hands and, radiant with joy, she will hold it up high, while singing a song she has heard, imitating it perfectly. The foam has to stay intact. She will even eat it. When it is time to get out of the bath she usually protests.

In general adults and children who show these characteristics are in good health. Some people have a tendency to get infections on the legs, nails or in the ears and easily develop a high temperature. Constipation and soiling often occurs, which is typical for this constitution. They often complain of headaches.

They are restless sleepers, sometimes waking up shouting and then falling asleep again. They usually wake up early, often hiding under blankets or pillow, but staying in bed. In the morning the bed will be in a complete mess.

They do not pay much attention to their physical care. Some people with additional complex needs will constantly make noises like growling, humming, crying or giggling. Their physical as well as their sexual development is often delayed.

Behaviour

Thinking and observing

Adults and children with this constitution are reasonably good observers and often appear to notice changes. However, they will not stay with things for long, as their attention tends to be dreamy and brief. The forgetfulness is usually related to the short-term memory. Their capacity to learn is much restricted by the extent of their forgetfulness and poor ability to concentrate, but their understanding and judgement are unrelated to this. Some understand a lot, but can hardly remember any facts.

A large number of people who are 'too forgetful' will develop an ingenious system to cover up their forgetfulness. Through all kinds of tricks they will find out what the time is or what is written in the book. Some read it on your face.

> Monique, (age 9, in Mental Health Care, TIQ 70, ASD), at first appears to be quite clever. She has moved to a new house. She plays nicely with the other children, but every time she has to go to the toilet she wants one of the other children to accompany her. This began to be seen as rather strange. She was good at covering up her forgetfulness. Fortunately it was understood in good time that she was unable to remember the way to the toilet.

Once familiar with this constitution you realize how much insecurity is hidden behind the façade. A boy of 12 says: 'I have read that word a thousand times, of course I know it.' This boy is very conscious of his problem. He is ashamed of himself and tends to get depressed.

People with these characteristics should not be confused with those suffering from trauma. In some cases the latter 'cannot remember' because memories that are too painful would come to the surface at the same time.

In contrast to people with ADHD, children and adults who are too forgetful have long-lasting interests and a good attention span. Their difficulties come to the fore most obviously in school. If you forget much or almost everything, you may still be able to learn to read, but arithmetic becomes quite hard and subjects based on factual knowledge like geography and biology will remain weak, in spite of the fact that there is a definite interest present. They can be very good at painting, drawing etc. It is also typical that even people with a more severe developmental impairment are often able to remember a melody straight away. After having heard a song only once they can sing it without any mistakes, sometimes at a high pitch.

Feeling

Unpredictable emotional outbursts are typical for this constitution. Children and adults with these characteristics will often come to you to tell you something with openness and lots of sympathy, sometimes in a slightly pushy way. At other times they can be irritable and have inexplicable outbursts of anger. They can be very impatient. If they want something it has to happen immediately. They are insecure beneath their restlessness, which they will express by their movements or by talking fast. They are unable to build on their ability to remember things, resulting in a poor sense of identity.

> Walter is 14 years old (learning disability, TIQ 60, ODD). He enjoys being outside and one quiet morning he is playing in the garden with some other boys. They are kicking a ball around. Walter picks up the ball which had fallen into the bushes and gets it ready in front of his feet. Another boy runs towards it and kicks it, also kicking Walter's foot. He explodes, cursing and swearing furiously, rips a piece of a wooden fence out of the ground complete with the post. It is full of nails and he starts to swing it around. Someone wants to stop him, but he shouts that it was not his fault, throws the wood away and runs out of the garden.

Apart from restlessness, there can also be dreaminess and passivity. Then you may see someone sitting on the side, all alone, staring into the distance with a somewhat empty facial expression or walking around aimlessly. There is great sensitivity to weather conditions and to moods. Because of their ever present insecurity people with this constitution tend to claim the attention of parents, support workers and peers. Although the adults around them provide support, this is by them sometimes perceived as oppressive. Contact with peers is pleasant but superficial. They are often very popular at parties and other gatherings. They prefer to play with younger children.

Their enthusiasm can be great at times. They may, for instance, be completely dedicated to the environment or to Greenpeace. They can be creative, full of initiative and originality. They can have imaginative plans while cleverly avoiding the necessary knowledge, and depending on slogans and actions.

Doing

People with forgetfulness also show a varying pattern of behaviour in getting into action. They may start something or join in with something full of enthusiasm and ideas and then suddenly lapse into aimlessness and passivity. It is possible to distinguish:

— Social people with a warm heart.
— Imaginative people with a tendency to compulsive thinking patterns and also bizarre fantasies (sometimes classified as having PDD-NOS).

> Stephanie (age 24, in Mental Health Care, TIQ 80 with disharmonic intelligence profile, ADHD) is bored and is walking around scolding others, yet she is charming to support workers and guests. She looks good, is well-dressed and well-groomed. She can barely read or do maths. She is fixated on earning money and dreams of marrying a nice man and having a house of her own. With much help and encouragement she manages to get a job in the bakery of a supermarket. For a while she is doing fine and everybody likes her, until after a while she begins to make mistakes in her work and will always ask others for help without explaining why. Stephanie notices that she has been 'found out' and she does not like the work any longer. Eventually she leaves after a quarrel. Her next step is in catering and there it goes well for a long time with the help of a computer.

People with forgetfulness will usually have problems with transitions and find it hard to go from one situation into another if they have not been told often and shortly before what is going to happen. Some people have problems with solemn, official and religious events and will become impatient. They find it hard to wait for their turn and may disturb the course of events, for instance, by screaming, spitting and making noises. These people do not have any inner speech and are unable to say to themselves: 'Just wait a minute.' In the book, *Omgaan met een dysfatisch kind* (*Dealing with a dysphasic child,* [not translated into English.*tr.*]) Riet Grauwel and Gerdi de Nooij explain that a lack of inner language will hamper development.

Not only the person with compulsive behaviour has compulsions, but compulsive behaviour may also be found in those who are forgetful. For clarity's sake we call their compulsions 'fixations'. One can see in most of these people that habits around eating, going to bed, leaving the house etc. become fixed or ritualized (as in ASD) so as to make sure that nothing will go wrong. Repeating the same action again and again, as in compulsive behaviour, is less pronounced.

Almost all those with the 'too forgetful' constitution love water: bathing, swimming, showering, playing with the tap, putting water into the mouth and walking around with it, playing with saliva or nasal mucus.

As for physical contact they will either like playing, romping, horsing around, or dislike any physical contact. Because of their naive openness they may be vulnerable to sexual abuse.

> Jennie (age seven, learning disability, TIQ 20, ASD) is very 'forgetful'. She is like a butterfly. She skips about all over the place with her slender figure, lovely with her reddish curls and dreamy look. She needs somebody with her to hold her hand all the time, otherwise she would never stop skipping. She does not speak and does not know her own name.

In everything a person with these characteristics does there is something fleeting and a tendency to let go and dream away. They are able to fulfil small tasks, although there is always the possibility that while doing this they will forget what they were doing. Things are usually done carelessly and will not be completed.

In those with this constitution aggression and self-mutilation (self-harming) may occur in various forms. They also tend to break things. They may be quite irritable and tense. They may be explosive and react quickly or lash out unexpectedly. Their aggression may be directed to those who are weaker and may then also involve them in their mischief. This occurs in various forms, from constant pinching to secretly or openly hitting and kicking. They may be prone to verbal aggression and might produce reams of swear words and insults.

Many are likely to run away. Some will walk off because they are in a kind of dream-state, looking for space and some because they feel hurt yet again and then like to take others along. If they are not too anxious, they may roam about for a long time and may make all kinds of superficial contacts.

Interpretation

People who display characteristics of this constitutional picture are often grouped together with people with ADHD or those with undefined learning disorders such as dysphasia. Dysphasia is described as follows: 'Dysphasic development corresponds with an expressive language disorder as described in DSM-iv (Diagnostic and Statistical Mental Disorders, 4th edition), but may also be categorized among the mixed receptive-expressive type. Dysphasia has not yet been recognized scientifically, unlike the expressive language disorder in the DSM-iv. Apart from speech problems, children with dysphasia may also have problems with motor control, known as "dyspraxia". "A distinctive feature of dysphasic development is a poor ability to memorize information, retention and finding of words."[14']

One often does not know how to deal with this kind of behaviour and will continually be searching for solutions. This is understandable, because this syndrome is not known in mainstream psychiatry. Forgetfulness is known in connection with the Korsakoff syndrome, dementia and brain damage.

The 'forgetful' person, however, is not understood or recognized, which is why they do not receive the correct support, in spite of the fact that there are concrete indications available.

This picture is more prevalent in children in mainstream primary schools than one might think! Could they be imaginative thinkers?

A person with forgetfulness has a poor capacity for remembering. From an anthroposophic point of view, memories are stored at the surface of the organs (the unconscious). If the surface of the organs is too compact and hard, mental pictures will bounce back, as happens in people with the 'too compulsive' constitution. If the surface is too soft, memories will sink down deeply as if into a swamp and become irretrievable. This is the case with those with the 'too forgetful' constitution. Everyone has a certain proportion of iron and sulphur in their constitution. These amounts have to be in balance. In this constitution there is too much sulphur in the organism, especially in the protein in the body (this can hardly ever be proven in mainstream science, but may be demonstrated via the so-called 'rising pictures')*.

The sulphur process is part of the metabolic process and of the way body cells are formed. Movement, heat, light and dissolving qualities will dominate if the proportion of sulphur is too high.

The surface of the organs where memories are stored contains too much sulphur in those with a 'too forgetful' constitution. Memories are, so to speak, sucked into it. They exist, but no longer rise to the

---

* As used in anthroposophic research into substances (tr.)

surface, in the same way as a tree is preserved in a swamp and does not rot because no air can reach it. Memories can therefore not be digested, resulting in unexplainable outbursts, inner tensions and irritability. Psychologically, this gives a feeling of powerlessness and a limited sense of identity. People will react to this in different ways, some with resignation and passivity, others rather by getting irritable and restless, showing the need for mental health care. The latter tend to remain much more dependent on their surroundings than they would like to be.

The high sulphur content also determines the colour of the hair and the pale, sensitive, often dry, skin. Those with such a constitution have 'incarnation' problems, and, in combination with their inner tension, this may lead to symptoms of constipation, encopresis (involuntary soiling), superficial sleep, headaches and hyper-sensitivity to light.

The dominating qualities of sulphur—warmth, movement and dissolution—explain the rather childish, open appearance and the waves of sympathy and enthusiasm.

It is very special that people with this constitution often have an excellent memory for music (also described by Oliver Sacks in his book, *The Man who Mistook his Wife for a Hat*). An explanation for this has so far not been found. We probably remember music in a different way from mental pictures.

Walter Holtzapfel writes in his book, *Children with a Difference:*

> What would the human being be without memory? A being without a history, living for the moment only; spiritually living from hand-to-mouth, metaphorically speaking. It is only with memory that continuity and coherence enter into life. It forms the basis for ego-consciousness.

Causes

The only known factor why someone has this constitution is that it appears at birth and is inherent in certain people.

Similar symptoms may also occur in someone with a brain injury caused by an accident.

Forgetfulness can also occur in people who have experienced severe trauma. The particular memories are so painful that they prefer not to remember anything at all.

Supportive approach

Motto: making things visible and using music.
Deeper fear: loss of identity.
Greatest longing: to have memories.

The most important guidelines for support are: order, repetition, stability, few stimuli, and music. It is important to assess the inability properly and not to blame people for it, but rather offer additional support.

In daily life
In relation to a supportive approach much may be gleaned from the above. It is not possible to simply remove or forbid someone's restlessness and tension. Treatment (e.g. balancing sulphur constitutionally) will take time and may not always be successful. Yet extra tension can be prevented by bringing structure and clarity into someone's life. Prevention of stimuli may be helpful as would be the regular provision of a quiet place as well as extra protection. This will prevent problematic behaviour.

Rudolf Steiner says about children with this constitution:

Now, let us consider such a fiery volcano, a child with high sulphur levels [...] The impressions that lie hidden within are a torment. We have to get them to the surface, not by psychoanalysis in the present sense but truly 'psycho-analytically'. ... Which things are vanishing in the child? [...] Things which the child does not recall should be shown to them again and again, in rhythmical repetition. You need to know what can really be helpful. [...] You can see excitement and apathy at the same time! They find learning very hard! And they can be rascals. As soon as the teacher walks away from such a boy's seat and leans over to another child, the boy suddenly comes up behind the teacher and hits him on the backside.....

Now you see, there are many of these children who show these traits to a greater or lesser degree. [...] Their power of absorbing external impressions is as a rule limited to quite specific kinds of impressions with a specific, typical character [...]. If you work in this way and have good ideas, such as building up a rhythm and speaking a verse together, then their protein will get out of the habit of being too sulphurous [...]. By bringing in something powerful from above we encourage the weak [metabolic] pole to be more active. ...In the Steiner Waldorf school this has become a general rule. It is all about giving a certain orientation in the direction appropriate to the child. We should learn to see the world imaginatively and not to think too much about it, but always be interested and observant. These people 'have to operate with only a few concepts'.[15]

People who show these characteristics need to be told what is going to happen next, what is expected from them, who will be there, what will change, etc. After some time they might be able to name or write down events that recur daily. Events need to be shown in picture form in a copybook or as pictograms on a large board.

> Roger (age 28 years, learning disability, VIQ 50, ASD) lives independently and a support worker visits him a couple of times a week. In language appropriate for him the support worker has made various computer lists of things he should or could be doing. With one mouse-click he can see them and this works well. If he has a question he can phone the support worker. He volunteers in a home for the elderly, bringing around the coffee. To entertain the people he will play the piano beautifully and sing all kinds of well-known songs.

Constant repetition may eventually work right into the organism (the etheric body), giving structure to it. Repetition is more effective if the same accompanying words are used every time. For this reason it is a good thing to make up little rhymes, songs or word sequences to be used by everyone. People with this constitution are able to remember melodies and lyrics or rhythmical, rhyming poems faultlessly (a form of memory from early childhood). Also when doing small tasks or fostering independence, little songs naming the sequence of actions could be made up, which the child or adult can then integrate and carry out.

Things in the person's environment must have fixed places, preferably accompanied by names and pictograms. It is a good idea if they walk by these things regularly, naming them and imprinting them on their memory. Fixed objects can be used as landmarks. You could also go for the same walk again and again, naming the things you see and letting them repeat after you.

If someone with such a constitution gets into a temper it would be better to allow them to let off steam first and to bring the matter up again only afterwards. It will be important to set clear boundaries afterwards and not to demand that they explain why it happened.

It can be helpful to stick to particular activities and then extend their limit every time by using a timer.

With sufficient support and security from their surroundings the demanding behaviour may well decrease. In general they should not be pushed too much, as they will not be able to sustain this because of their inner tension.

Vulnerability is a recurring theme here. Sometimes their childlike trust goes too far and they will have to learn through regular training that certain situations can be dangerous or are simply 'not done'.

Nutrition

As is the case with the 'too compulsive' constitution, much may be achieved with a 'too forgetful' constitution via nutrition.

A dietary list may be found at the end of this chapter. On this list all kinds of indications are found that can be applied in daily life. A lot can be achieved in various ways. We know, for instance, that one boy's restlessness and irritability decreased by drinking a cup of broth every morning. Giving them a carrot instead of an apple after school or sharing out more or less food at dinner time are some examples of how the diet could be implemented.

School, workshop

In addition to the pedagogical indications in the home life, in school the learning process will demand much extra attention. Forgetfulness will often cause the pupil's achievements to lag behind. It is especially at school that the obstacles become more prominent and the child will need much support and understanding. It can be helpful to draw pictures with words and short stories and to look at them again and again. It is also important to use a method of learning and working that centres around constant repetition and a lot of music. Even then gaps may appear leading to a diagnosis of 'learning disability' among others.

Supportive measures

— *Medication*
General (anthroposophic) medication: Ferrum, Pyrites, Scorodite, Veratrum D4.

— *Eurythmy therapy*
Working with consonants among other things.

– *Art therapy*
Here it is important to be aware of elements of form and of the principle of repetition.

– *Healing environment*
Create a clear and consistent structure in the surroundings, e.g. by way of named signs, pictograms and arrows. Use colours that are clear, cool and not too light.

– *Music therapy*
Use melody and rhythm and then introduce language to support verbal memory.

– *Play therapy and conversation therapy*
These therapies are not relevant here.

– *Therapeutic speech and regular speech therapy*
Here too the elements of repetition and form are important, as they stimulate the incarnation process.

– *Cognitive behaviour therapy*
This can be very helpful for children and adults with an IQ over 50 and age 10 and up.

– *Family therapy*
This is very important. There is often a lack of understanding for people with this constitution.

Diet lists

Drawn up by professional nutritionist Mirjam Matze:

Diet list for the sulphur-rich diet
For the compulsive constitution the emphasis is on the sulphur-process.

Foods:
— Preferable for grains: millet, barley, oats, buckwheat and oat groats.

— A lot of fruit, raw or cooked.
— Nuts.
— Seeds (sesame, sunflower, coriander, cumin, caraway, anise, dill, mustard).
— Sweeteners: honey, raw cane sugar, concentrated fruit-juice, malt-syrup, apple-spread, jam.
— Dried fruit: (raisins, currants, prunes, apricots etc.).
— Fruiting vegetables: pumpkin, gherkin, courgette, cucumber.
— Flowering vegetables: cauliflower, broccoli.
— Salads of lightly steamed vegetables.
— Seasonings: sambal, soya sauce, tamari, pepper, curry, mustard.

General preparation methods:
— Sweet, sour or spicy tastes can be predominant.
— Moderate amount of raw vegetables.
— Make ample use of oil and butter.
— As many hot dishes as possible, if necessary also with the lighter meals.

Where possible avoid:
— Root vegetables (carrots, beetroot, celeriac, parsnip, black salsify, Jerusalem artichoke, kohlrabi, horse-radish, radish etc.).
— Kitchen salt, marmite, bouillon powder.
— Beet sugar (white sugar).
— Golden syrup.

Diet list for the iron-rich diet

For the forgetful constitution the emphasis is on the iron-process.

Foods:
— Preferable grains: rye, corn, wheat.
— Root vegetables: carrots, beetroot, celeriac, parsnip, black salsify, Jerusalem artichoke, kohlrabi, winter-radish, radish.
— Sweeteners: beet-sugar, golden syrup.
— Seasonings: marmite, kitchen-salt, bouillon powder.
— Herbs: lovage root, parsley root.

General preparation methods:
— Use salty, bitter and astringent flavours.
— Salads may be prepared with plenty of raw, fresh (not preserved) vegetables.

Where possible avoid:
- Fruit and dried fruit.
- Fruiting vegetables (tomato, peppers, pumpkin, gherkin, courgette, aubergine, cucumber.
- Flowering vegetables (cauliflower and broccoli).
- Seeds and herbal seeds (sesame, sunflower, coriander, cumin, caraway, anise, dill, mustard).
- Cane-sugar, honey, malt-syrup, apple-spread, jam.
- Nuts.
- Sambal, soya sauce, tamari, pepper, ginger root, mustard.
- Horse-radish, ground ginger.

5
Constitution Type 3—Too Congested

An example

Graham (age 13 years, learning disabilities, TIQ 70, ASD) is coming with me to a separate room. He just had a terrible outburst in the classroom, because one of the other boys told him that the 'Ajax' football club could easily lose a match one day. He jumped up straight away, roaring and swearing furiously, trying to attack the boy. His teacher just managed to pull him off, but he did not calm down. He continued to wave his arms wildly and kick to free himself, roaring like a lion. Once outside the classroom, he calmed down somewhat but went on yelling: 'I will beat him up soon. I will kill him!' As a precaution and to his dismay he is being held by his sweat-soaked T-shirt until inside the room. When given paper and coloured pencils, he nevertheless grabs a black pen. With great intensity he draws all kinds of animals, mostly snakes. Then he uses the pen as a knife to chop off their heads. He adds in a fury: 'I'll chop off your head, serves you right.'

Outer appearance

When observing the outer appearance of people who show characteristics of this constitution, you will find four different types (see below), so not only one recognizable appearance. The heavier type can be found more often, especially in people over the age of ten. These people make a somewhat compact and impenetrable impression. Physically this shows most clearly in thick, dry or flabby skin, which does not feel enlivened by healthy interaction with the environment.

It is typical for this constitution that it rarely gives an impression of being inwardly light and radiant, apart from straight after a temper or outburst of anger; otherwise there is usually a certain dullness or heaviness.

Below are the four types according to their outer appearance. One of the life processes is disturbed due to the inability to cope with a particular element:

— athletic, muscular, compact, heavy, poor blood circulation, low body-temperature (element of fire);
— slim, tall, sinewy, rigid, disturbed balance (earth element);
— light, graceful, slender, agile, disturbed consciousness, irregular breathing (air element);
— stocky, not muscular, plump, flabby, slow, feelings of nausea, urge to vomit, (water element).

Movement, posture and motor skills

We will address movement, posture and motor skills in a general way. See 'Posture' for the variations according to type.

Movement

The movements are generally heavy, rather than quick and light. This could also be caused by medication. The more able amongst people with this constitution keep up easily with others when playing football but this is more related to 'pushing power' and rough kicking than speed and skill. They lack motor coordination to a greater or lesser degree. They will often bump into things or knock something over. In sports their learning disability can present limitations.

When hammering or chopping they tend to hit too hard and will often miss. As long as the heaviness is not predominant and they manage to get into action, they can be very strong and will persevere: in no time they will have dug up a patch of land.

> A young woman (age 22 years, TIQ 50, attachment disorder) has a tendency to gain too much weight. Now she weighs much more than the average person of her age. Her constitution is 'too congested'. From the moment she herself decided to change this situation, however, her will has been strong. She will only eat a little and sometimes even spit out the food.
>
> As a young child she had many traumatic experiences. EMDR (*Eye Movement Desensitization and Reprocessing*) helps her to actively resume the thread of her life.

Her sense of balance is poor, which became obvious when she was learning to ride a bike.

People who show these characteristics often have difficulties in traffic. They usually need a tricycle because their sense of orientation is poor. They may suffer from unexpected fluctuations in consciousness through which they are often unable to have an overview of the situation in good time. Learning to swim is often very hard, especially to begin with to dare to float. They often fear letting go of the ground under their feet.

Posture
You can also recognize the congestion in the posture. The shoulders are hunched, the chin juts out tensely, hands are clenched into fists or the back is arched. Somewhere in the body there is pent-up tension, although the intensity varies. The same disharmony may almost always also be found in their speech, as speaking requires an even more subtle and precise control of one's own movements. The phenomenon of congestion can be seen in stuttering, pausing between words, exaggerating the enunciation of the plosives, speaking too loudly with hardly any melody in the sentences and speaking monotonously.

Motor skills
Fine motor skills, as needed for writing for instance, are poorly developed. It can be learned, but more slowly than usual. You may occasionally come across people showing these characteristics who have well-developed fine motor skills. Restlessness caused by congestion may often be found in the movements as well as clumsiness and bumping into things. There often are problems with balance. You may see tics, persistent movements like stamping the ground with one foot, twisting buttons or locks of hair, especially at moments when the congestion is increasing.

Life processes

Hardly anyone with this constitution is happy in their body. They do not really wake up properly in the morning and are as if stuck somewhere in the process of waking up (see also the paragraph on 'Interpretation'). In a manner of speaking they are always in a bad-morning mood. Things are quickly too much for them and they can become irritable. They feel uncomfortable for no particular reason. Stress and energy within their body cannot break through, causing inner pressure and tension. Sometimes they can accurately describe this feeling, for instance, as 'a kind of fireball inside the stomach'.

They can be insensitive, or rather hyper-sensitive, to areas in their environment and in their own body. In some, and sometimes in all of the life processes, you can see a disturbance in the healthy exchange with the environment. Depending on the type (see above) they are constitutionally unable to integrate one or several of the elements (earth, water, air and fire).

It is important to learn to recognize the indications of physical congestion, so as to be able to prevent a temper tantrum or an epileptic seizure.

Possible indications comprise:

— irritability, listlessness;
— pale skin colour;
— restlessness, walking around in circles, different tics;
— twisting buttons or a lock of hair;
— showing the whites of the eyes, dribbling;
— making smacking noises.

Waking up fully as well as going to sleep and letting go can be difficult. Generally, however, they will sleep like a log and it is hard to wake them up. Waking up may be more of a problem for some people and falling asleep for others. Experience has shown that people with this 'congested' constitution are more restless at full moon.

> Tanja [age 41, learning disability, TIQ 60, diagnosed with M(ultiple) C(omplex)D(evelopmental)D(isorder)] is a passionate person with a tremendous amount of energy, enthusiasm and fierce temper tantrums. When this happens she is usually taken out for a run. Occasionally she will have an epileptic seizure. She lives in an institution and a co-worker found out one night that she was fighting with the moon. At half past two he was woken up by sounds from outside, screams and footsteps on the gravel. He looked out of the window and saw Tanja standing in the light of the full moon with a big stick in her hand hitting out at the moon, with an angry face and swearing.

As to sexual development it appears that in puberty youngsters who have a lot of subconscious inner tension feel an almost unconquerable urge to express their sexuality. It is hard to restrain them. This is less so with people who are more dreamy.

Behaviour

As is the case with the other constitution types, the phenomenon of 'too congested' occurs on various levels of development, ranging from a poor to a reasonably good ability to learn. This book is about adults and children with moderate to severe learning disabilities.

It is well-known that anti-epilepsy medication may strongly influence behaviour.

Thinking and perception

People with this constitution usually have no or little idea how they come across in social life. There seems to be a kind of deafness to this. In some it may go so far that they do not learn to discern between 'mine and thine' or even 'she or he' or 'woman or man'. They often display a strong fascination with money.

> Bernard (age 16, with mental health problems, TIQ 80, PDD-NOS) goes to the swimming pool with some peers. Everybody is in the water but Bernard is nowhere to be found. He has only dipped his toes into the water, as he usually does, and then disappears into the dressing rooms, which he meticulously searches for coins. Also in the library this is his favourite activity, and with his huge body he will crawl along the carpet, feeling under all the bookshelves.

Their self-reflection and self-knowledge are not very good. Discussing this is usually quite hard, not because of a lack of will to understand, but because of an inability to do so. This does not mean that the observation skills as such are poor, but that the ability to concentrate and to achieve things vary.

They often have particular subjects or hobbies that interest them. Here they can apply themselves with enormous willpower and persistence and are then able to achieve a lot. Then they may have great ideas and boundless ambitions, while losing sight of reality. They usually pursue these interests on their own.

> A woman (age 21 years, Mental Health Care, TIQ 100, epilepsy/ personality disorder) with a very forceful character would write the most beautiful

poems when feeling a kind of relief in the moments after an epileptic seizure. She had learned to play the violin well and everybody around her liked to hear her play. She wished to perform on the big stage in the future. She was, however, only rarely able to play together with someone else and keep in time with them.

People with this constitution, even the weaker ones among them (with a mild learning disability), can come out with wise words, which show that they have profound insight into the world around them, yet with (too) high ideals. Having these flashes of wisdom seems to be a gift and is not something that develops gradually. It comes to the fore at unexpected moments, especially when they feel free from the congestion after an attack. They will integrate this wisdom into their life of feeling or into their actions to a varying degree.

Watching a movie or television may increase the congestion due to the loosening effect of the rapid flashes of light.

It took a long time before a link was established between epilepsy and certain types of behaviour, but in 2007, after research, mainstream health care determined that behavioural problems occur in children with epilepsy.[16] Earlier, Dr Sanders-Woudstra wrote:

> It has already been stated that children with epilepsy display more behavioural problems than other children. Frequent issues are hyper-activity, poor concentration, poor listening skills, mood swings. Children with psycho-motor seizures may have ictal (ictus= attack) symptoms such as hallucinations, depersonalization, derealisation, delusions, panic attacks, or a particular gait reminiscent of a transient state of psychosis. Prodomal [pre-psychotic, tr.] mood swings, with apathy, irritability and aggression, may precede a seizure and may last from a few hours to several days.[17]

Feeling

Frequent mood swings are characteristic for people with this constitution. One moment, they may approach you with enormous enthusiasm and rather forcefully—for instance by speaking loudly—and share an experience with you. The next moment they may react irritably and sullenly. The difficulty with these mood swings is their unpredictability and this is also a problem for themselves, as they are the most bothered by it.

Whether in a bad or a good mood, they will demand a lot of attention. They do not have much of an ability to gauge what the other person wants or does not want, which often leads to them being diagnosed as being on the autistic spectrum.

They are often restless and irritable. They easily get stuck and then want to get their own way with great stubbornness and perseverance. It is very hard, if not impossible, for them to be flexible and to let go. They often need help, whatever the situation may be.

> One morning, Sandra (age 12, Mental Health, TIQ 80, ASD) came to breakfast with bare feet. The group leader asked her to put on her socks and shoes. Sandra may not have noticed that she had forgotten something, despite usually being quite alert. She felt caught out and exposed to the other children. She refused and called the group leader a rotten fish. When he insisted, Sandra started to hurl things around and someone was called in to help. Sandra was completely stuck in the tantrum and continued to yell and scold, be it now in her own room. Eventually she calmed down when someone quietly put her slippers on her feet. Suddenly she became aware of her feet again and the bad mood faded away. Things began to flow and the congestion decreased.

The younger the person and the more severely the disability, the more they prefer to be close to a carer or support worker. They will follow that person everywhere and can only let them go with difficulty in order to do something by themselves. Emotional pressure, dramatic events and anxiety may increase the congestion and therefore also the disturbing behaviour.

They often suffer from bad nightmares full of menace and horrific images. The latter will also appear when they are playing, as their imagination is rarely light-hearted and joyful. They will often break things while playing. Someone with this constitution can suddenly fly into a rage and smash up everything around them, because their inner tension has got out of control.

Socially, such a person may sometimes badger and irritate others while losing sight of anything else. They do not really have any idea how this affects others. The uncomfortable sensation they live with is trying to find a way out and the strong reaction of the person they are badgering may provide the wakefulness they are looking for.

> Jacob (age 46, learning disability, TIQ 60, MCDD) works on a farm. Whenever he does not feel so well, he starts swearing. Also passers-by on the public road can be targeted. There is no way to stop him, however

much one tries. In the end calling in the police has a temporary effect. He likes to work with sheep and is good at it. He will calm down completely when he is with these animals.

At other times they can be nice, get on well with others and will try to make friends. This is done in such a clumsy way that it is rarely successful. They often look for friends among people with negative behaviour, and will join in with it because they are attracted to them.

Doing

With regard to their actions, you may see strong fluctuations in people with this constitution. They often look pale and listless, and seem to be suffering from an undefinable physical discomfort (congestion).

At other times they will start something and then there will be quick and strong activity. They are capable of enormous activity and extreme exertion. They may easily chop ten times more wood than another person of their age, full of enthusiasm and unstoppable. If they are not fully awake or close to a seizure, this enormous strength may switch to dangerous aggression or blind rage, which one should not attempt to restrain.

> John (age 8, learning disability, VIQ 40, ASD) has regular seizures, in spite of a high dose of medication. Whenever he experiences the congestion within his body, he becomes fidgety and will beat the ground with one foot. If nobody pays any attention to him, he may take a large tricycle, ride away out of the gate into the sand dunes, or he may go on to the road and begin to walk along the white line in the middle until he is stopped.

One can often see that again and again there are times that they are not quite 'with it' when doing something: their movements slow down and they keep repeating the same movement. Often what is needed is some encouragement, to be woken up or called upon. If you see something they have written it will strike you that one or more characters will sink below the line or be stretched out, showing how their consciousness fluctuates.

Er stond een appelboom

Some show spiteful behaviour like biting or hitting. Often it is necessary to impose clear consequences to get through to them (wake them up) and to make them stop. During a 'good period' this kind of behaviour may disappear again like snow melting in the sun.

The following passage from *The Idiot* by Fyodor Dostoyevsky describing one of his own epileptic seizures, illustrates the feelings of someone with a 'congested' constitution.

> .... when suddenly amid the sadness, spiritual darkness and depression, his brain seemed to catch fire at brief moments, and with an extraordinary momentum his vital forces were strained to the utmost all at once. His sensation of being alive and his awareness increased tenfold at those moments, which flashed by like lightning. His mind and heart were flooded by a dazzling light. All his agitation, all his doubts and worries, seemed composed in a twinkling, culminating in a great calm, full of serene and harmonious joy and hope, full of understanding and the knowledge of the final cause. But those moments, those flashes of intuition, were merely the presentiment of the last second (never more than a second) which preceded the actual 'fit'. This second was, of course, unendurable. [Translation by David Magarshack, Penguin 1953]

Interpretation

People with these characteristics are also frequently diagnosed with ASD and MCDD. Congestion as a phenomenon can only come about when a force or energy is obstructed.

What is obstructed in a person with a 'congested' constitution?

Someone with a healthy body is not hampered by this body, but is able to use it. They will 'get through' and then be able to perceive and sense their environment and themselves, and act without any great obstacles. In a person with such a congested constitution the wakeful, conscious functions are, to a varying degree, repressed by the physical body. It is possible that such a person may display self-harming behaviour. They want to wake up, often with great determination, but are unable to. This will then cause congestion of formless energy in the organ in question, causing unpleasant physical sensations.

> The rhythm of the reversal of the metabolic process between going to sleep and waking up is disturbed. Before a seizure certain metabolic substances will accumulate in the blood. The seizure will then release these substances like a thunderstorm after a hot, sultry evening.[18]

Sensations of inner pressure and tension, feeling too full, trapped and irritable will frequently occur and will, to a certain degree, obstruct mental capacity.

Why are the wakeful (astral) and conscious ('I') elements unable to 'get through'? According to Rudolf Steiner in *Education for Special Needs,* this is caused by one or more organs having become hardened, insufficiently warmed through or too dense. This situation may be congenital or could have been caused by an accident, often due to brain damage.

The organ in which the congestion occurs is not necessarily diseased or clinically proven to be abnormal. This may make it hard to determine which organ is involved. Indications may be derived from looking at the four types described above. (See under 'Supportive approach', below for the organs concerned.) Some physicians will measure an accumulation of warmth (congestion) in an organ.

If the congestion has become too great, release will follow in the form of an epileptic seizure, a temper tantrum or aggression. The force of the accumulated energy is so great (enough to light a small lamp) that consciousness may be switched off or decreased by it. The person may have a seizure, or attack whatever comes in their way with enormous strength, far greater than is normally possible. This strength is charged with destruction. Only after the discharge will there be a shorter or longer period of tranquillity, extreme exhaustion and need for sleep.

According to Wikipedia, the cause of epilepsy is still unknown. Scientific research suggests that epileptic seizures are caused by a disturbance in neuro-transmission.

Causes

— Hereditary predisposition, i.e. a number of characteristics of this constitution have been present from birth.
— Brain damage and scar tissue on the brain; sometimes epileptic seizures will only occur after some years.

— Severe neglect, traumas resulting in hardening of the etheric body.
— Vaccinations.
— Encephalitis, streptococcal infection, cerebral infarction or brain haemorrhage.
— Chronic alcohol and/or drug abuse.
— Poisonous substances, psychoactive drugs.

Thirty percent of people with a learning disability have epilepsy.[19]

Supportive approach

Motto: waking up.
Deeper anxieties: getting locked in, exploding.
Deepest longing: breaking free.

From the phenomena one can glean where consciousness is unable to break through. Supportive measures are directed to these areas so the impenetrable place can be incorporated into a flowing wholeness.

By understanding the full picture you can learn to observe to what degree a child or adult struggles with a disability, and therefore is not simply annoying, irritating or stubborn. Without this insight, dealing with the demanding, often negative behaviour is a difficult task for those surrounding them. For support to the four types with regard to clothing, nutrition and dealing with the life processes, see the diagram below.

Element	Organ	Phenomena	Supportive approach
Heat, fire	heart	Poor blood circulation, low body temperature	Dressing just a little too warmly, so that the person almost perspires. Movement aids warmth
Air	kidneys	Disturbances in consciousness, irregular breathing, bloating, hyperventilation	Carefully guided breathing exercises, speech exercises, ball games, running, playing flute or trumpet

| Water | liver | Feelings of nausea, tendency to vomit, perspiration, much saliva | Learning to swim, stimulating the sense of taste, preparing food in a varied way with herbs; painting, modelling |
| Earth | lung | Disturbed balance, heavy gait, falling over, dizziness | Balancing and dumb-bell exercises, gymnastics or eurythmy, apparatus work, movement, jumping, carrying heavy things, cutting branches |

If it is not clear where most of the disturbances are situated, any of the exercises can be applied. The balancing exercises and encouraging perspiration have proved to be most effective.

Seizures can be provoked by strong sense impressions, circulation problems, food intolerances, sensitivity to the moon and the weather, disturbed sleep, disturbance in the everyday life rhythms like eating etc, as well as the misuse of drugs and alcohol.

Daily life

Apart from the above exercises, which can of course be varied endlessly, you can learn to be alert to moments in daily life when the child or adult withdraws, switches off or loses concentration. Especially these short moments, that occur frequently and always require an adequate response, are more important than a single therapy session every week.

The moment the person 'switches off', they have to be 'called back' with a clear voice. This can be done in various ways: calling their name, clapping one's hands, changing the subject, making a joke, touching them, playing around for just a short moment. You do not have to be too careful, but make sure not to frighten them. The aim is to constantly keep them 'with it', thus preventing congestion and allowing the organism to gradually become more permeable. This will be more effective than talking. It is a truly healing therapy.

Showing irritation has an adverse effect, as it will make them withdraw and cause tension to build up. The best thing would be to state what has happened, to name everything and definitely not to address their emotions, as this could increase the congestion or the aggression.

Independence

Activities and tasks should be clearly defined and simple. You have to consider that everything will only slowly get through to the person and that they will only be able to slowly put into practice what you have asked of them. Steps towards independence have to be small, otherwise disappointment will follow again and again. Children and adults who show these characteristics tend to overestimate themselves.

Activities, play

It is a good idea to stimulate the senses in a positive way as this will improve alertness. Here one could think of the senses on three different levels: *the physical senses,* with which we perceive physical sensations that are usually subconscious; the *middle senses* on the feeling level, directed to experiencing the surroundings, and the *higher senses,* especially active in the social domain.[20]

The *physical senses are:* sense of touch, sense of movement, sense of balance, sense of life.

The *senses of feeling are:* sense of taste, sense of smell, sense of sight, sense of warmth.

The *higher senses are:* sense of hearing, sense of word, sense of thought, sense of the 'I'.

In order to encourage alertness and release congestion, it is helpful to enable vigorous *physical* activity. Sawing and chopping wood, carrying heavy things, pushing a wheelbarrow filled with bricks, digging etc., are wonderful activities here and will help people feel better afterwards. Of course this is also the case when going for long walks, cycling with a backpack, or swimming a good number of laps. Other possibilities are blowing up balloons, blowing into a straw or at cotton wool, clay-modelling, horse play, weightlifting, doing push ups, putting chairs onto tables, boxing, all kinds of sports etc.

By means of all sorts of games and observations the *middle or feeling senses* can be stimulated. This can be done more forcefully (with sounds, flavours, colours, heat etc.) than with others, without the risk of startling the person. As flavours one could use: mustard, salsa and grapefruit juice.

The *higher senses* can be stimulated by keeping the person continuously alert and by teaching them social skills.

In particular those who show negative behaviour—like bullying, stealing, calling names—need to continuously hear what is allowed and what is not. They themselves have little or no notion of this due to their lack of awareness. There should be clear consequences to their deeds: if you do this, this is what will happen. These consequences must be carried out with a neutral attitude, without using too many words but consistently, so that the person gradually begins to realize what the environment wants or does not want. The disturbing behaviour will then usually cease for a while.

> Fred (age 26 years, TIQ 80, ASD) had for some time been taking a number of things from the shops in the village. One day someone told him very clearly about the consequences of this for the shopkeepers and for himself. He woke up and went to all the shops to give back the stolen goods and to apologize.

Taking away the person's favourite things is not very effective as this will often increase their negativity. Consequences of anti-social behaviour should, however, be clearly felt, e.g.: going to one's room for five minutes, doing an extra job, or doing something positive for others. It is helpful to implement such a sanction immediately as soon as it has been agreed upon, so they will grasp the meaning of it.

When telling stories to children or adults it can be very effective to include their problem (tension, feeling threatened) in an unrecognizable form, exaggerating it. Choose an age-appropriate theme.

School and the workplace

Many of the measures that can be applied in the home life could also be used at school or in the workplace.

Within the protective environment of a classroom or workshop extra attention can be given to the development of social skills by encouraging friendships and by letting the child or adult do things for others. These activities may also promote the acceptance of the child or adult by others.

There are various ways of helping the person to be alert at school and work:

— By doing group exercises in observation, reacting quickly and with alertness.
— By drawing exercises that demand much consciousness.
— By language exercises in which certain elements have been left out, so the person has to watch out and is kept alert.
— By much movement, gymnastics, sport.
— By doing work that demands alertness and/or physical effort.

Also in the classroom or workshop a person with this constitution may display varying degrees of concentration and mood swings. The teacher or workshop-coordinator should bear these in mind and observe them quietly without paying too much attention, so as to prevent the person from manipulating their environment.

Supportive measures

— *Medication*

Anthroposophic medicine can help set in motion organic processes that have become stuck. In this context it is possible to take as one's starting point the four elements as outlined in the above diagram. The physician could also give nutritional advice. General medicines: Sulphur, Belladonna, Copper, Hyoscyamus.

Allopathic medication may be necessary where the person is at risk due to frequent seizures. Nowadays medication can be adjusted very precisely and will generally have the effect of diminishing stimuli in the brain. Adverse side effects may be: drowsiness and not being able to experience a feeling of liberation after a seizure.

— *External therapies*

Organs in which there may be congestion can be treated with wrappings, oil applications ('Einreibungen'), or compresses. Massaging the calves with rosemary can help a person feel their body. Various types of baths can increase the circulation. Special wrappings can induce perspiration. Treatment of kidneys, liver, heart and lungs can decrease the seizures.

– Physiotherapy
In physiotherapy one can work with balancing exercises, breathing exercises and exercises with heavy weights like dumb-bells in order to release some of the congestion. Swimming and trampoline can also be included.

– Eurythmy therapy
Among other exercises, doing many 'E' exercises whereby the legs and arms are crossed vigorously to encourage wakefulness. Also exercises to promote circulation, consciousness and balance.

– Art therapy
Painting and clay-modelling are ways to practise working with the elements of water and earth respectively. This therapy can help enhance alert observation. Through drawing exercises one can attempt to open up fixed, closed forms and to make them more fluid, and through form drawing one can call on the person's consciousness. 'Let them get used to strong stimulation by light and sound[21].' Keep them busy all the time.

– Healing environment
The environment must be inviting and stimulating as appropriate. The light must be bright; colours: yellow and orange.

– Music therapy
The trumpet or the crumhorn are often played for or by people with this constitution; these instruments demand a good breathing technique. Rhythm and consort playing can help increase listening and concentration skills.

– Drama therapy
Those who are older can learn to give form to their ideals. Adults or adolescents will be confronted by themselves whenever they have overestimated their possibilities. Learning to put oneself into another person's place has a healing effect.

– Play- and conversation therapy.
This could be helpful if there are problems with acceptance and a negative self-image, but must not be used to act out dark fantasies.

— Anthroposophic therapeutic speech and regular speech therapy
Possible speech defects as well as breathing can be addressed by these therapies.

— Cognitive behaviour therapy
This can be very helpful in treating children and adults with an IQ of over 50 and over 10 years of age.

— Family therapy and family support
Family therapy may be very helpful for practising social functioning and developing awareness for each other's abilities and inabilities.

6
Constitution Type 4—Too Open

An example

No one has ever seen him (age 16, learning disability, TIQ 30, ASD) put his head on the pillow when in bed. His head does not touch the pillow, but is one centimetre above it. Nobody knows if he ever really sleeps. Whenever you enter his room he is always awake.

During the day he tends to protect his head. When it is too noisy or too bright, Leo (age 48, low IQ) will put his long, thin arm over his head so it reaches his other ear. He tends to twist his other thin arm as well as his legs in a most complicated way, his head bent over and his eyes almost or fully closed. He seems to have closed himself off completely, yet many impressions still reach him. Bringing some kind of order into them and somehow processing these impressions is a full-time task for Leo.

Outer appearance

The outer appearance of people with this constitution manifests in two main groups. Many people are similar to Leo (48 years old, with an intellectual disability) and come across as tender and fragile. Their build is fine and slim, beautifully proportioned and finely shaped. You can see their veins and bones right through their thin, pale skin. They have long hands and feet, with tapering fingers and toes. They usually have straight hair and often have a kind of glittering in their eyes.

Other people with the 'too open' constitution, on the other hand, have a sturdy and chubby build. They look rosy and healthy, by far not fragile and tender. Their hair is usually not straight, but wiry and curly.

Posture, movement, motor skills

Posture

The extreme vulnerability mentioned above shows in the posture. There is a reluctance to being exposed. The shoulders and chest are contracted and the head is bent. People with these characteristics often sit somewhat hunched up, sometimes with their arms around themselves or even over their head, their legs pulled up beneath them or all cramped up and intertwined. They will protect themselves and their attitude is one of mild withdrawal. At the same time they are cautious and alert, the opposite of being relaxed.

The posture of people with the second set of characteristics initially appears to be not as vulnerable and they like to be in the foreground, but if something is asked of them they will withdraw and adopt an insecure, dependent or even aggressive attitude.

Movement

They appear to move with care and in a somewhat wooden way. Many people appear older than they are, especially those over the age of ten. Children below the age of ten show more suppleness and also restlessness in their movements.

They will often walk on tiptoes or in a bouncy way. Sometimes you may see them stop and retrace a few steps. Before crossing a threshold they will often hesitate or linger. Transitions are always difficult. They are not good at sports and gymnastics, mainly because they lack the courage and inclination to get fully involved. For example they may be scared to cycle fast, to run or to jump. They will avoid a ball or a fellow player coming towards them.

Once they have been helped over the threshold and have got started surrounded by their mates, those with some of the second set of characteristics tend to throw themselves rather wildly into things.

> Harry (age 27 years, in Mental Health Care, TIQ 80, ASD) tells enthusiastically about his work on a sheltered farm. He prefers to work in the wood-workshop, but he himself says: 'Also here I often just chat. I do not really like hoeing, because then I have to bend down too much and get a backache; shovelling compost is too heavy for me. I love painting; at first

the paint would run off the paper, but now, after a few months, I manage to keep it dry.'

Peter (age 24 years, Mental Health Care, TIQ 100, with a borderline psychosis) will dance to loud music when home from work. He does this in order to feel his body again.

Motor skills

Once they have put their mind to it, their fine motor skills are good or even ingenious. They can make the most beautiful things in hand-work, crafts, art and ceramics and they often manage to learn to play a musical instrument. They usually dislike sports and gymnastics together with others, as there is too much commotion and noise. Sometimes they will throw themselves into it with ambitious passion and little overview.

Those who are 'too open' and have a sturdier build do not move as cautiously, but rather somewhat ungainly. Their entry will not go unnoticed, as they will announce themselves with a loud voice and then throw themselves down somewhere. Both their gross and fine motor skills are somewhat slow and clumsy.

Life processes

In the first group the breathing is usually not deep, but rather high up and superficial; sometimes asthma may occur. They have problems falling asleep; they tend to lie awake for a long time, get out of bed often and be anxious. Once asleep, they will sleep deeply and in the morning it is hard to wake them up. Partly as a consequence of this and because by day they are often too stressed to go to the toilet, they tend to remain incontinent for a long time.

They are fussy eaters and will fish little bits out of their food or tea turning up their nose at it.

Annie (16 years old, Mental Health Care, VIQ 80, ASD) is a sensitive, pretty girl. She has difficulties to become more independent in the world. She always ate little and would quickly become constipated. In the end, as she has not been able to go to the toilet for days, she had to be admitted to hospital.

People with this constitution are usually slow eaters; in the morning they often have problems eating anything at all, as they are then not yet quite within their body. Some tend to drink a lot.

They often have diarrhoea or a sore stomach. Sometimes they become obsessed with small wounds which they will scratch open repeatedly, yet they may not feel it when they have a serious wound on the knee. They tend to catch colds or flu and be easily tired, but they hardly ever have a high temperature. They often complain of headaches (maybe because they do not want to go to school or work), but nonetheless they experience it as a reality. Their hands always feel clammy and moist and their feet are almost always cold. Various allergies and asthma are among other problems that may occur.

They have a thin skin which can easily lead to eczema. Some people may get startled even if you only touch them gently. In extreme cases they cannot bear wearing clothes. In good times they will enjoy being touched or hugged gently, as long as it is on their own terms.

Often they cannot bear other people's smell.

They are not really warmed through and in winter they may quickly look blue with cold.

The open constitution also shows in extreme perspiration (a 'flowing out'), especially at night, and in the morning there may be an unpleasant corpse-like smell in the room. Nail-biting also often occurs. In adults one may find a craving for hallucinogenic drugs.

The more robust people are less fussy with food and can have high temperatures. They easily retain too much fluid and are less easily cold. They fall asleep quickly and will sleep deeply. Physically and sexually they are precocious and active, while the first group lags far behind in these areas.

> Janie (age 12, in Mental Health Care, TIQ 80, ASD) was physically mature by the age of 12. She always liked to cling to people. She still prefers this to standing alone. As she is so open, she is well aware that boys are attracted to her. This fascinates and excites her. She does not know her boundaries and only realizes what is going on when (sometimes) it is too late. For this reason she remains vulnerable, although her behaviour may look like manipulation.

Behaviour

Thinking and perception

Many people with this constitution have a keen power of observation and are quite intelligent. They are so open that impressions affect them deeply. Harsh colours, sounds and other impressions literally hurt them and they cannot cope with them (Hypersensitivity Syndrome). These impressions can cause complete panic and they can feel overwhelmed by them. Their perception is geared so much towards their surroundings and so little to themselves that they will often perceive much more than we do: they may suddenly express what you are thinking, or will already 'know' about events that are still to come.

Sometimes they may perceive so much in their surroundings that they do not hear or see what is nearby. A little girl with this constitution was registered at a kindergarten as deaf, but very soon it became clear that she heard everything perfectly.

Due to emotional vulnerability the intellectual capacity may not always be fully developed. This may also be linked to a diagnosis of learning disability.

> Eric (age 10, learning disability, verbal IQ 40, ADHD) has quite a small and frail build. He seems to need all his energy to stay on his feet. When spending a somewhat longer time together with other children everything becomes too much for him. He does not manage to indicate that he wants to be left alone. Instead he will boss the others around with a loud, commanding voice, trying to make them stop bothering him. This will inevitably lead to fights or to more chaos.

People with these characteristics can be ingenious, often holding on to one or two themes about which they seem to know everything (ASD 'savants'). As is the case with those with the 'too compulsive' constitution, certain themes will occur frequently, such as the world of the stars, computers, music or technical subjects, or any other clear and objective subjects about which one can find out a lot. They do their research on their own. They can be extremely fascinated by tables and numbers, as these involve a clear framework which they can hold on to. This is different from compulsiveness in which there is an inability to forget a mental picture.

They have a very good memory, especially for things that have made a big impression on them or have hurt them. Those with a 'too open' constitution usually have a well-developed sense of smell and will feel uncomfortable in a room or near people with an unpleasant smell. Some will indulge so much in nice scents that it becomes pure physical enjoyment. You may see some people with more complex needs go around sniffing at all kinds of things and other people. Their hearing is keenly perceptive as are all the other senses. Well-executed live music gives them great pleasure.

Feeling

Because of their openness and profound vulnerability to impressions and stimuli, people who show these characteristics may easily consider themselves to be victims. They are extremely self-centred as a way to protect themselves and feel that the world and the others around them are always annoying them, causing them to be irritable. 'They are always teasing me, it is all too much, I need peace and quiet.' They have poor self-awareness, self-experience and self-reflection.

Due to their openness they will often be anxious and insecure in social life and reluctant to get into action. They tend to look to adults for security by constantly forcing them to pay attention to them.

> Diana (age 24 years, learning disability, TIQ 50, ASD) has been given the task of helping the gardening team at a sheltered workshop. Every morning all the participants will sit together to exchange experiences and to hear what they will be doing that day.
>
> Then everybody gets up to go to work. She also gets up but will then as a rule go to the toilet. When the group is ready to leave, she is still on the toilet with the door locked. Asking, begging, rewarding or forcing her will not be of any use. She will stay where she is, because she cannot cope with the chaos and the transition.

In the presence of their peers they may easily feel insulted or insecure and will then withdraw or avoid contact. Sometimes they make friends with people who are weaker, younger or ill. They may develop a strong attachment to animals, because animals are no threat to them. They are able to wholeheartedly care for animals or feel compassion for their suffering. Socially, however, they will boss others around, so as to avoid any chaos with which they would not be able to cope. They can often be very dominant. They are poor losers and things are never 'their fault'. They always know other people's weaknesses and tend to get at them where it hurts most whenever they themselves have problems, driving their environment to despair.

Because of their sensitivity they have a fine aesthetic and artistic sense; they will immediately hear if a tone is out of tune and notice when colours do not match; these things bother them. They enjoy genuinely beautiful, pure forms.

Also morally they long for purity and they have a keen sense for justice. In spite of the fact that these feelings are usually directed at themselves, they can feel sincere compassion for others and for the sorrows of the world.

In their imagination they tend to be extreme. They may be fascinated by morbid themes, but will at the same time also be fearful of them. Such themes may be accidents, blood, illness or death. Although unable to cope, they will be at the forefront of quarrels or social dramas and will be familiar with rumours. They are inclined to always find just the person who will hurt them. In the themes of their drawings you can often see how much they are affected by threats from the outside world.

They also fantasize about everything they could do: becoming a 'star' or helping to rid the world from suffering and war.

Those with such a constitution need much support in all areas; their fixation on this resembles compulsion. Their great vulnerability causes them to demand ever more security and to tyrannize their environment, often by making a scene. Outside their familiar situation they often manage to adapt and behave perfectly, but not without great effort. Once back in their familiar surroundings they will revert to their previous behaviour, unseen by others apart from the people nearest to them.

Children and adults with the 'too open' constitution may come up with wise expressions, showing insights far beyond their age. At other times this wisdom will disappear again. This wisdom is not their own, but they sense it.

Doing

Children and adults with this constitution find it hard to get going and, if they do, it often does not turn out as they had wanted. This will cause great disappointment about themselves, but especially about everything that goes against them. They will shout: 'I can't do it anyway', and will then tear up their work or throw it away and may hit themselves out of fury. They do not manage to persevere. This may cause them to lag behind in the learning process, especially in relation to their own performance. It is then hard to motivate them again to continue. They rarely have any idea of their own part in this.

Encouraging them and giving them clear, simple assignments below their level are absolutely essential. Their basic attitude is: 'I want to, but I cannot do it. Yet I have to do it and if I do it, it will turn out differently from how it should be and so it is never really right.' Having to make choices is very hard for them and they may be wavering for ages.

They can be very demanding to the people around them. Trying to get them to do small tasks may lead to serious conflicts or aggression, especially if they are demanded or forced to do something, as there is a fine line here. Some will direct their aggression towards themselves in the form of depression, self-harm, suicide or refusing to eat (psychiatric problems). They will cut themselves off from their environment.

At other times they may offer to help you with something and will do this skilfully and quickly. In a safe environment they are well able to amuse themselves and produce the most beautiful things showing great originality and skills in all kinds of areas. Then they will learn quickly in the area of crafts, drawing, painting, music as well as in other skills. They can make beautiful drawings, recognizable by their minute, exact shapes with not much colour. Alternatively, their drawings may be so large that they barely fit onto the paper. They also like to dress up in costumes designed or made by themselves and will then pretend to be someone else. They will either act on their own or want to be the main character. As mentioned above, they like to choose particular themes and hobbies which they can work on alone and which have a kind of intrinsic order.

> Melanie (age 39, Mental Health Care, TIQ 50, schizophrenia) had already from early on been able to knit, embroider and weave beautifully. She preferred to do this on her own with an adult nearby. When she herself became an adult an ideal workplace was found for her. In a workshop where musical instruments are built she is in a room partitioned off by glass and varnishes the instruments, an activity which demands great skill. She can do this better than anyone else.
>
> George (15, Mental Health Care, VIQ 70, ASD) is always busy on his own after school. He builds one wooden box after another, with big heavy

locks. Half a year later he learnt to do pottery. He likes to continue until late after all the others have left and will then make beautiful vases.

Those with this constitution will tune in with others ('astral body') so readily that they can mimic them exactly and also imitate their way of speaking perfectly. They do this without actually being aware of this themselves. They will pick up so much from others that they sometimes appear very capable, but will not have made these skills their own. If they do not feel secure and protected, they will shift their attention unconsciously to others in their surroundings, thus managing to enhance *their* disturbing behaviour.

Interpretation

From the previous chapter it became clear that a person with a 'too congested' constitution has a physical blockage, hindering them from freely making use of an alert consciousness. The astral body and the 'I' are partly held back because one or more organs are cramped or hardened. The opposite is the case in people who are too open or 'flow out' too much (this syndrome is sometimes called 'childhood hysteria'). The physical make-up is too permeable, which, among other things, manifests in phenomena like a thin skin, eczema and excessive fluid loss. The body does not provide a firm basis for thinking, feeling and doing (astral body) and for consciousness ('I'). Today the phenomenon of 'hyper-sensitivity' is becoming more well-known and, in my opinion, this phenomenon coincides with the 'too open' constitution type.[22]

Out of a sound impulse people with this constitution will look for experiences that may help them find themselves by dramatizing, manipulating, self-mutilation, demanding attention or trying to hold onto something. This behaviour in itself does not provide solutions, but becomes understandable against the background described above. Letting go of their physical foundation too soon may also explain why they are so often preoccupied with themes like illness, accidents and death. (Borderline) psychosis may occur.

This constitution causes poor awareness of concrete reality and causes adults and children to be unable to take hold of themselves; sometimes they become paralyzed by panic (being unable to speak, eat or walk).

The openness will often remain as great as in very young children, causing them to protect or isolate themselves. Here a connection with autism may be found. In many people with ASD the underlying cause may well be their 'too open' constitution.

Dissociative disorders too may also occur in people with such a physical foundation, over and above lack of protection or traumatic experiences.

Causes

A 'too open' constitution may originate in:

— Heredity.
— Educators whose emotional life is too much in the open.
— A symbiotic relation, that does not allow any independence from the educator to develop.
— Neglect, poor development of the life processes.
— Traumatic events such as incest or abuse. This may have been passed down from generation to generation. Consequences may be: fear of identification with one's own body (dissociation), lack of trust in one's own physical foundation, guilt feelings.

Supportive approach

Motto: providing a skin.
Deeper fear: falling apart.
Greatest longing: finding oneself.

The basic attitude in dealing with a person with 'too open' characteristics should ideally comprise:

— A protective, sheltering approach, without any direct confrontation.
— Emotional stability, keeping a reasonable distance, not allowing oneself to go along with strong emotions, be they positive or negative.
— Predictability; no sudden changes in approach.
— Few stimuli.
— Helping the person along, taking the first steps together.
— Rewarding positive achievements in a quiet and consistent way.
— No judgement if they 'are unable to do' something.

In the life sphere

It is of essential importance for such a person that in daily life there is order in events and in their environment. A fixed daily and weekly programme, manageable and clear to the person concerned, will help create predictability and a sense of security. This programme must be adhered to, not severely or with confrontation and coercion, but by always calmly and clearly repeating what is going to happen. It is advisable not to give in to any attempts, even those accompanied by big scenes, to cross boundaries or to make the carer cross their own boundaries. Picture cards are very effective and objective.

> In a bakery, large pictures demonstrate the sequence of actions that have to be performed. This has helped one baker, a person who is 'too open', to be able to work more independently. When he comes into the bakery he can see what has to be done. This is also done for children in school: their task will be waiting for them on their desk.

If the programme has to be changed unexpectedly, children or adults with this constitution should be informed in an understanding way. Although they can often express things clearly and know much, they find it hard to make choices; it is good not to give them a choice between more than two options. The possibility of making small choices may be a step towards taking more responsibility.

They are quickly bothered by commotion and chaos. Giving them a quiet place at certain times will have a positive effect, as only then they will be able to relax properly. Sometimes certain rituals or reassurances will be needed in order to make this possible.

Some group leaders working with a group of children told me that children with this constitution love being rolled into a blanket at certain times of the day. People who show such characteristics may easily feel rejected and find it hard to let go. They will also keenly feel any hint of irritation or coercion from the support worker. It is helpful to always keep them in mind to some extent. Sometimes this may mean holding their hand or doing things together; or it may suffice to look at them every now and then and say some encouraging words. In this way the support worker will provide a kind of *skin* to the person and will thus prevent anxiety and dramas. This will be the more effective if all those supporting this person will together form such a skin. The tragedy of this constitution is that support in the sense of a 'cure' is very difficult. The fact that a person is so poorly integrated in their body, and therefore 'excarnates' too quickly, is more difficult than having a delayed development.

Yet sometimes, with much patience and perseverance, they could be helped to recognize and manage their own patterns. It is important to keep working on this with youngsters and adults.

Waking up

— Children and adults with this constitution will usually wake up early, especially in the summer. It is a good idea to teach them to stay in bed and rest. (Once in puberty they often like to go to sleep late, especially children with a heavier build.)

— Give an immediate and careful explanation and preview of the day. If they are having a hard time, comfort or encourage them, speaking quietly, whispering and humming.

— Help the person to get going, then let them gradually do more on their own (every beginning is hard and may be painful).

— Limit stimuli as much as possible; being woken up too quickly makes people vulnerable and may ruin the day; if necessary let them eat alone. Young people and adults can decide this for themselves.

— Their skin needs natural protection, which tends to get rinsed off in the shower. For this reason an occasional bath should suffice.

— Faking illness to get out of school or work? An occasional rest day before it comes to this would be a workable solution.

Nutrition

— Avoid sweet things; sugar has an 'excarnating' effect (pulls you out of your body) and is hard to digest. Fruit, raisins and honey could be given.

— Also grains, muesli and brown bread, but not too many products that are hard to digest such as fats, red meat, pork and raw food.

— Salty and sour products like sauerkraut and rhubarb are good because they have formative and astringent effects. Salty and sour products (e.g. salty snacks and liquorice) can also be used in between meals or as spreads on bread.

— Broth, marmite, oranges.

— No hot spices such as mustard, pepper etc.

— Camomile and lavender tea.

Clothing

— Literally provide them with an 'extra *skin*' in the form of several layers of clothing: cotton vest, woollen vest, shirt, jumper, tights, woollen socks, sturdy boots or shoes.

— Make sure that clothes have a tight fit and can be felt against the skin. They often cannot tolerate wool against their thin skin. Use natural materials for the absorption of moisture; if necessary fabrics made of peat fibres can be used. Change socks frequently. For outside: a good, warm coat, hat, gloves and scarf. The colours should be nice and not too bright or too many.

— Care for the skin with warming, protective oils, creams or lotions.

Independence

As became apparent from the above there is usually no lack of skills, but rather of endurance, courage and motivation. It is important to find a task that does not cause any thresholds, so it is good to start at the lowest level. You have to prepare such a step so the person can visualize it, thus lessening their fear for the unknown.

To get the person going it is helpful to join in at the start and then go along with them. A good sequence of events for this would be: putting your hand on their hand, putting your hand on their arm, keeping your hand behind your back, then standing behind them and, after that, staying nearby. The reason why this works is because with them an impulse does not reach their muscles and will therefore not be translated into action. Someone else is needed to help establish the connection ('Facilitated Communication').

It is helpful to reward them excessively after they have achieved something; after all, they are 'princes' and 'princesses' and are 'special'. This approach is quite efficient. When they have social problems you could ask them to play the role of a knight or a queen, doing good work and protecting others.

When they get older it is necessary to support them in getting to know their fears and learning to cope with them. They can also learn to keep an eye on their health and get to know their weak areas. They will generally need support and encouragement for a long time.

Activities, play

The sensitive, artistic side of the person with a 'too open' constitution, as well as their own particular 'themes', will already partly indicate possibilities for hobbies, play and work. They do not like bravery, sports, physical accomplishments and lengthy activities involving many others. They would rather stay home or near home (watching birds, flowers etc.).

Dick (age 17, TIQ 70, ASD), one of the bigger boys in the institution, has learnt computer skills. Within a short time he has become very good at it, as if through a kind of sixth sense. He has become more skilled than his teacher. He likes to walk around one of the offices, where there is always someone having difficulties with a computer program: then Dick will come to the rescue.

Let them have a sheltered place for their hobbies, where they can get on with things. Help them along first, after which you could encourage them regularly. Give them nice materials in beautiful colours, for they deserve it. They need storybooks in which fear is overcome by courage.

With younger children it helps to sing a lot, do finger games and other movement games. This will give them confidence as then they are touching their body in a matter-of-course way without any direct demands. Young people and adults could write down their experiences in a secret diary.

For all those with this constitution it may be very beneficial to care for something or somebody in need of their help. They like this and will do it meticulously; it will cheer them up and give them energy. Sometimes you will hardly recognize them.

They are not very keen on board games, but it could help to occasionally encourage them to join in so they can learn to stand up for themselves, play fairly and learn to cope with losing.

Supportive measures

— Medication
The skin could be strengthened and the digestion supported with medication. General medicines: Bryophyllum, Silver, Oxalis (in cases of trauma), Iron and Mercury. Sulphur for skin problems.

— External measures
External measures, such as oil-applications ('Einreibungen') or compresses, may be quite effective for strengthening the skin and the organs and for the experience of their own body. Solum Uliginosum and hypericum oil.

– Eurythmy therapy
This can help transform their movement patterns from being 'too open' to becoming more closed, which may also affect them right into the organs and may help overcome bed-wetting, among other things.

– Healing environment
Protective and gentle environment, for instance through cushions and separate corners. The colour light-blue providing space and protection. Dim lighting. Order.

– Art therapy
Through painting learning to deal with the fluid element. Learning to fill in a white page by oneself, which takes courage. Learning to create harmony through colour and form which they themselves long for so much. Modelling with clay often demands too much strength, but beeswax is pleasant to work with, as it has a warming effect and one can make nice little figures with it.

– Music therapy
People who show these characteristics usually love music. The clear, objective laws of music are healing to them, both in listening and in playing and singing. Some musical instruments may get them into action and help them learn to develop perseverance.

– Play therapy and conversation therapy.
These forms of therapy are especially advisable for older adolescents in the process of learning to deal with their own reality.

– Cognitive behaviour therapy
This may be very helpful for children and adults with an IQ of over 50 and over 10 years of age.

– Family therapy and family support
This is often necessary, because coping with people with this constitution is usually a complicated task for family members.

7
Constitution Type 5—Too Heavy

An example

Hello, who are you and where are you from? This is how this person greets us in a friendly and open way. It is a recurring experience when entering the premises of an institution for people with learning difficulties. If you then start a conversation, surprised by this interest, it appears that it basically does not go any further. There was not really any need for a deep conversation or replies, apart from on a very basic level. Nevertheless an atmosphere of trust was created which will prove to be lasting. It was a disarming encounter brought about not by exchanging information, but by creating a pleasant mood and the feeling that your presence counts.

Everyone is greeted in this way without any discrimination as to norms or values, but with a true openness, something that is rare in our society.

Outer appearance

People with the traits of the 'too heavy' constitution can especially be recognized by their movement and posture.

It is actually not easy to characterize the outer appearance, although the body is often stocky or overweight. A slender, tall build will occur less frequently. (People with the particular physical characteristics of Down's syndrome are also among this group.) 'Heavy' is not a description of a person's weight, but rather of their gait.

Movement, posture and motor skills.

Movement
Slow, heavy movement, that can often already be spotted from a distance, is typical for this constitution. Getting into movement takes some effort.

One can observe a lumbering gait and the whole upper body being somewhat bent over.

> Saskia (age 22 years, in Learning Disability Care, TIQ 40) works in a small grocery shop at a day centre. She was asked to put potatoes from a crate into 500 gram bags. She dutifully filled the bags and kept working without stopping, urged on by the seemingly endless stream of potatoes on the assembly line. Suddenly there were no bags left, but she kept putting and squeezing potatoes into the last bag until it broke. She then called for help and it took quite some time to explain to her what had happened.

All movements are more or less slow and heavy, as if not moving through air, but through a denser substance. Also running appears to be slower. You may sometimes see people with this constitution move more quickly, but only when they are still young and have a clear aim. Once they are in movement their circulation seems to get going and then they are able to persevere for a long time and may even walk 15 miles or so.

Posture
Heaviness is predominant in the posture. The shoulders and head will be bent over and sometimes the mouth is open. The arms will be hanging heavily down alongside the body. The posture rarely presents an image of wakefulness (apart from in those with a mild learning disability): they will often sit bent over and slouching, with their head in their hands. The description given above may be recognized at various levels. In some people you will find it in a mild form, in others it is more pronounced.

Motor skills
The gross motor skills are poorly developed in people who show characteristics of this constitution. They are not keen on physical education. Jumping is hard or impossible for them and they have great problems keeping their balance. (In children and adults with Down's syndrome one may find hyper-mobility which can make the impression of agility.) Not all succeed in learning to ride a bicycle or to swim, although once they have got going they will be able to keep up a continuous, rhythmical movement for a long time, for instance when going for a walk.

The finer motor skills are often especially slow, yet some people can be quite skilful. Jobs like setting the table may take a long time, as may getting dressed or sweeping. It also usually takes a long time to learn these things. Drawing, writing, handwork and crafts usually demand great effort. Some people in this group appear to be good at handwork, crafts, writing and reading, but their pace remains slow and their power of abstraction poor.

Slow development of motor skills is typical. In babies there is a delay in lifting the head, sitting and grasping, as well as in standing up and walking. Speech development will be delayed or will not happen at all. Later on, if speech has developed, it will remain slow with a smaller or larger vocabulary, depending on the level of intelligence.

> Simon (age 28, TIQ 80, P(erformance)IQ 100, ADD) works together with a group of peers doing odd jobs. He has an excellent grasp of all kinds of technical problems and likes to help. He talks just a little bit more slowly than his peers. They notice that he is different. They tease him and, being of a gentle nature, he cannot understand why. As a consequence, every time he is asked to do something at home he has started to behave aggressively, sometimes almost dangerously so. There too, things are sometimes going too fast for him, although his understanding and ability are good. The parents are seriously thinking about a temporary solution in the form of admission to an institution.

Life processes

Metabolic disorders occur frequently in this group and are the most common cause of this particular constitution. A large variety of metabolic disorders may occur, such as stomach pains, constipation, diarrhoea and food intolerances e.g. to fats, sugars or dairy. In winter, there may be frequent prolonged colds and runny noses, as well as eye or ear infections, causing sensory problems.

The breathing is shallow, not deep as would be expected from the prevalence of heaviness and slowness. This proves that the slowness is not caused by laziness but by a disorder.

People showing the characteristics of the 'too heavy' constitution do not like to stay up late in the evening. They have trouble waking up in the morning and are slow to get going. When lacking physical exercise, they will tire quickly and get cold hands and feet.

Their sexual development is normal or will be somewhat delayed. Masturbation occurs frequently. From the age of 20 or later healthy loving relationships may develop.

Behaviour

Thinking and perceiving

Although people with this constitution have good sensory abilities they are slow to react to stimuli. Movement from within outwards is delayed. Sometimes an appropriate reaction will only come after a few minutes, hours or even days, but is then not recognized as such and is therefore discounted. The support workers of a girl without any speech who needed much help with her basic care needs only noticed after a long time that she would quietly giggle about subtle jokes among the support staff, although they did not think she was able to understand them.

A slight delay in speech, understanding, thinking, learning, reacting and getting going may also be observed. People who show these characteristics often have trouble putting into words what they see or experience, if they can do so at all. This is why they are often diagnosed with ASD. If they show any thought processes in relation to outer connections, they will be slow to get going. Their capacity for imagination and orientation remains limited. Depending on the level of development, some people may develop the capacity for abstract thinking.

They can generally remember concrete events, especially festivals or events that recur on a regular basis and will enjoy talking about them. They will not often talk about the future.

They may suddenly wake up to certain things. This is different for each person.

> Brigid (age 8, learning disability, TIQ 20, ASD) does not speak or seem to make any contact with the carers or anyone else. Her daily occupations are sitting on a swing boat or rocking on a chair, seemingly oblivious of her surroundings. On a walk she prefers to hang on to someone's arm. Sometimes, however, she will suddenly disappear within a split second and is then nowhere to be found. Then it turns out that she has spotted a glistening sweetie paper or crisp packet in the bushes, apparently without having looked for it. At home she might snatch a biscuit so fast that nobody will notice.

If one can keep them moving, people with this constitution will remain more awake than before and will be able to express themselves and understand more than at other times.

Feeling

A beautiful quality in people with this constitution is a remarkable awareness of their self-worth. They definitely do not want any help if it is not really necessary.

They also have great social gifts, although these may go unnoticed. As described above, they are naturally openminded in a way that is unparalleled. Irritation, impatience and discontent from those around them, however, sometimes frustrate this talent causing anger and aggression.

Those who have looked after or supported people with this constitution over a longer period of time will know that they will often give you a hug when you most need it. They also know how these children and adults can comfort others who are having a hard time, mostly without many words. They are not actively involved, but may, for instance, sit quietly next to a peer with autism for hours, with the result that the person relaxes and is content. They sense much of what is going on socially.

They are not very good at verbally expressing their emotions. When they are down and you ask them what the matter is, they will often respond with a standard reply or none at all. They do not seem able to become conscious of their emotions sufficiently or quickly enough. Sometimes they manage to a certain extent, but only after a while.

> A young woman (age 17, learning disability, TIQ 40) who comes across as somewhat slow and dreamy, will sometimes suddenly burst into tears. When asked what the matter is she will respond: 'I don't know.' After more persistent questioning she will often say: 'I am homesick.' If you then ask her if she wants to go home she says: 'No.' Confronted with this contradiction she will look at you helplessly and not say anything else.

One should not confuse a person with this constitution type with someone with depression. People who have a tendency to depression are also 'heavy', but with an additional gloominess and inaccessibility, which is not the case with the constitution described here. A combination of depression and being 'too heavy' may occur, especially if such a person who is 'too heavy' has been met with a lack of understanding for a long time. This will usually mean that too much is being demanded from them without it being noticed that their slowness is causing them problems. Self-harm may be a consequence of not being understood.

Doing

Although people who show characteristics of this constitution tend to move slowly, they love movement. You will often find them in places where people come and go. They always know when there is a nice atmosphere or when there is a visitor. They love parties, drama and music. They like to play host or hostess (or a different part) and can be good imitators. They love making music (music is also a form of movement) and may pick up a lyre or guitar or sit down at the piano and sing. You can often see quite some repetition in their activities. They can enjoy themselves immensely and radiate happiness. They usually like something nice to eat. This may get them moving faster than you would have expected. They love doing things for others. Once they have learned, with some help, to do small chores in and around the house, they will do them faithfully and keenly.

> A boy (age 18, learning disability, TIQ 50, Down's syndrome) enjoys working in a little shop. He fills the shelves in a certain area in the shop. He does not say much, but does his work carefully and slowly. A boy of the same age who goes to a secondary school and helps in the shop every Saturday once offered to help him so things would speed up, but he was given the abrupt reply: 'I can do it myself.'

Trying to hurry them on, rushing or pushing them is of no use. It would be a mistake to think that they are lazy or unwilling. They will react with stubbornness, rejection or aggression; the latter will occur especially in people who have been talked down to again and again. They will either play up or not do anything at all any longer. In some cases they may become depressed or self-harm.

In relation to movement we frequently see people with this constitution and a low IQ rock or move from side to side, either in standing or kneeling, while grinding their teeth, sucking their hand or something like this. Playing with sand or marbles, endlessly letting them flow between their fingers is a favourite occupation. With this they bring about the outward movement they themselves are so sorely lacking.

Interpretation

Reading the above, one might think: aha, this is a person with a learning disability, brain damage or Down's syndrome... These are well-known terms that are commonly used, but what exactly do they mean? People with developmental and behavioural issues were not taken seriously for a long time. Barely any attention was given to their mental well-being. Their problematic behaviour was thought to have been caused by their learning disability. Within the last decades this has changed drastically. There are continuous discussions whether to place certain people in Mental Health Services or in Learning Disability Services.

We are here using the term 'too heavy' for a particular reason. The term 'too heavy' relates to the movement of the limbs and to the life processes, where, according to medical pedagogy inspired by anthroposophy, the central disturbance in people of this constitution type is to be found.,

When studying the sequence of developmental steps in young children, one can see that speaking and thinking only start because the metabolic-limb system (motor system) has been set into motion.

Nowadays medical science knows of many metabolic disorders that lead to insufficient brain development. The well-known neonatal 'heelprick' is given to new-born babies in order to prevent a certain metabolic disorder (phenylketonuria). If this disorder occurs and remains untreated it could trigger developmental delay.

Many metabolic disorders are related to inadequate or delayed breakdown of proteins. So far, research has shown the existence of around 5000 different metabolic illnesses. In those suffering from such a disorder, metabolic processes are providing a weak foundation for the developmental activities of the will and of movement and also for speaking and thinking. There will be a continued delay of movement in the limb system and the processes of consciousness will get going too slowly, too late and not strongly enough. The brain will not develop fully. This 'getting going' is not a one-off event in small children but is set to remain. From the above it becomes understandable, that although the person with a 'too heavy' constitution does receive stimuli—because there is nothing wrong with their ears, eyes, and other senses—they will, on the other hand, show delayed reaction and will come into movement slowly. 'Delayed mental development' may seem to be an adequate term, but actually appears to be incorrect, because the point is that the chemical processes in the *body* should be adequate.

> Philip (age 34, learning disability, TIQ 40, Down's syndrome) is roaring with laughter. Someone has just told him that there is a power cut in his house. The coffee-machine, the electric kettle, the computer and the telephone are not working. This is something that always happens within his body, and now others have the same problem.

Processes of consciousness allow a developing person to learn to be more objective, have opinions and individualize their emotions. We see that those with this constitution will do this to a lesser degree, thus retaining social qualities (the open, non-discriminating attitude mentioned above) that get lost in so-called 'normal' development.

Now it becomes clear why, once in movement, they will show an alertness that cannot be called upon at any other time.

> Although experience and dominance can stimulate the growth of the brain and the reinforcement of the synapses, prolonged helplessness will affect the brain. Already for this reason we should try as much as possible to coax the person away from their passivity and dependency. This can be done by promoting their independence.[23]

Causes

— Metabolic disorder resulting in delayed brain development.
— Brain damage, e.g. encephalitis.
— Alcohol or drug abuse by the mother during pregnancy.
— Chromosomal aberration (such as in Down's syndrome).
— As a consequence of intra-uterine lesions (scarlet fever, toxoplasmosis).
— Extreme neglect, shock at a very young age.

Supportive approach

Motto: providing a purpose.
Deep fear: stagnation.
Deepest longing: movement and flow.

When working with a person who shows these 'too heavy' characteristics it is important to *mobilize* thinking, feeling and will, both in individual support and in supporting them in daily life and school. Provide them with a purpose which will especially enthuse them. This enthusiasm will help them overcome their heaviness. Then one could draw up a plan for an activity. After the activity they could be made aware of their achievement by rewarding them and reviewing it. In this way the educator makes use of the underlying cause of this constitution.

Their resistance and stubbornness when encouraged originate in an inability (slowness) and not a lack of willingness. In case of aggression: lower the demand and do not use any pressure. They are basically quite willing and have an open, trusting attitude.

Always give them ample time to get used to new things or changes and prepare them thoroughly so they can begin to look forward to it and will join in willingly. Humour is of the essence. Those with such a constitution usually like being touched gently. Also this may get them moving. If there is excessive masturbation, it may help to divert their attention and offer them a possibility to do physical activities.

Daily life

A fixed and regular daily programme is very important in the day-to-day activities; the order of the day should be clear and familiar, but not rigid.

Waking up

— Open the curtains quietly.
— Go along with the heaviness for a little while and then get them into action (start from where they are).
— Help with the initial movements.
— Let them run up and down the corridor or let them stamp their feet.
— Wash their whole body with cool, salty water (which has a stimulating and awakening effect) or with rosemary, or let them take a quick shower (not too hot) to stimulate the blood-circulation. Then rub them down well.
— Rub rosemary oil on calves and feet.
— Give them a clear overview of the day to come in a joyful and light way.

Nutrition

— Not too much starchy food, sugar or porridge.
— Stress lightly astringent tastes such as broth, lemon juice, marmite and food with rough fibres such as wholemeal bread and raw food, in order to stimulate the digestive process.

— Make sure that the digestion works as well as possible and, if there are problems, adapt the diet (prunes, fennel, and a lot of water to drink) or give medication.

Clothing

— Make sure the person is dressed warmly, but not too warm.
— Pay special attention to keeping the hands and feet warm; if they are cold it will be hard for the person to get going.
— Use natural fabrics that breathe and do not shut off.
— Touching and/or rubbing them warm throughout the day can be helpful; they will then become aware of their body again, flow will enter and they will be able to experience movement.
— It is important that clothing and shoes are not too tight or irritating, as this would lead to unhappiness and a refusal to do things. Sometimes they themselves are unable to indicate what is bothering them.

Independence

Give them short, bite-sized instructions easily understandable to them. Do this with enthusiasm and with the promise of an attractive aim or reward at the end, for instance by saying: 'If we do this, so and so will be happy…, this and this will happen.' Always repeat the instructions in the same way, in a clear sequence and one by one, so they can become habits and do not need to be grasped intellectually. Only give instructions for activities that are directly related to normal, everyday life. Pictograms are very useful here.

Start with doing tasks together, then next to the person (imitation) and then let them do it partly on their own. Try and use clownish jokes, in which everyday things go just a bit wrong, as if by accident. This will wake them up, make them laugh (flow), and they will then join in.

Activities, games

— First get them moving in various ways and then try and stimulate their enthusiasm. Walking, cycling and swimming with their continuous movements are favourites.
— Also any kind of ball games, children's games, playing on the swing (not too long), roller-skating, playing at marbles, playing tag, hide-and-seek. In the more complicated games they will often miss the point, but will run along with the others.

— In the work situation, pay attention to movement and meaningfulness for the person. Do not let them work on their own, as then they will often slow down or stop.

— Movement may be stimulated for children also in the home: building with bricks, playing with cars, rolling balls over the floor, singing games with actions or passing things around. Games or exercises with the feet or involving touching the body are very good. Making music, dancing, singing, drama, puppet-shows and similar activities are especially valuable for all.

— Many people are unable to follow movies and television as they move too fast. Some can do craftwork and handwork independently. Usually, they enjoy doing useful tasks like setting the table, cleaning, cooking and other small jobs.

— The most therapeutically effective stories are about events from daily life, clearly and elaborately described, enabling people to use their imagination. They will easily grasp short, recognizable stories describing animals, some jokes or something nice to eat, preferably told with drama and gestures.

— In the evening it is good to try and review one or two events from that day together, so their memory is stimulated.

Supportive measures

− Medication

A lot can be done to support the life processes. Anthroposophic medication can stimulate the processes of warmth, light and movement in the body. If need be, the metabolism can be improved by means of medication and nutritional advice. Medication for general use: Triticum preparation, Apis Regina comp., Kephalodoron, and, in cases of depression, Aurum with Hypericum.

− External therapies

External therapies, such as massage, oil applications and therapeutic baths, may be used to help increase warmth and circulation in the body: oil applications on the spleen and the liver, and Levico and lemon baths.

– Physiotherapy
To stimulate movement and enhance awareness of the limbs.

– Eurythmy therapy
There is an indication to work with the sounds R, L, S, I ('ee') to stimulate movement, flow, direction and body awareness. This is the fundamental sequence for a person who shows characteristics of the 'too heavy' constitution.

– Healing environment
For those with this constitution the environment must be ordered and practical, but also homely, light and inviting to movement or to the observation of movement activities.

– Artistic therapy
In art therapy one could use wet-on-wet watercolour painting in order to learn to deal with fluids and to master flow. The emphasis should be on mobility and forming concrete pictures.

– Music therapy
Rhythm-instruments and the chrotta or cello can stimulate movement and circulation. Self-expression through singing. Moving to music has an energizing effect.

– Drama therapy
Drama can be helpful in learning to express oneself and to give form to inner experiences.

– Play- and conversation therapy.
Play- and conversation therapy can be helpful where there is frustration, trauma or depression.

– Anthroposophic therapeutic speech and mainstream speech therapy
By means of games and movement, speech therapy can help stimulate the more subtle speech movements and aid articulation. This may then have an effect on the further development of the brain.

– Cognitive behaviour therapy
Cognitive behaviour therapy may be very helpful in treating children and adults with an IQ of over 50 and over 10 years of age.

– Family therapy and family support
Family therapy can be very useful in helping family members to understand them and to learn to develop a positive way of being with them.

8
Constitution Type 6—Too Light

An example

'I will do that job for you,' he says helpfully. Jesse (age 19, Mental Health Care, VIQ 80, ADHD) is muscular but slender. He never sits still and always has a plan that has to be executed. He is already on his way with long bouncy strides, his upper body leaning forwards and his head even further forwards. He is going to help dig a hole for a pond. He loves doing heavy work. 'Just a minute, Jesse, we first have to think how we are going to do it, so put your spade down over there for a moment. The hole should be 50 cm deep and this is the circumference. You can put the sand over there in a heap.'

'OK,' says Jesse and the spade is already in his hands again. 'Are you going to measure it?'

'Oh yes, stupid me.'

He is given a tape measure, with which he has some previous experience, or so he says.

'Just show me how you do it.'

Then Jesse shows how he wants to do it. He gets new instructions and repeats them to himself.

Then he gets to work. It is going reasonably well and after some time he continues by himself, but for no longer than five minutes. The heap looks very high. Jesse is standing inside the hole up to his middle.

'How is it going, Jesse?'

'Fine, nice and deep, isn't it?'

'How deep, Jesse?'

He sets the measuring tape at the bottom of the hole and calls out triumphantly:

'Fifty centimetres, exactly! Oh, yes, I forgot to look there, at the top. I can easily fill it in again,' he says and happily sets to work again.

Outer appearance

Children and adults who show characteristics of this constitution type are generally slim and muscular. Fair hair and blue eyes often occur, but by far not exclusively.

There are also people with this constitution and ADHD who have a sturdier and fuller appearance. Restlessness occurs much less frequently in them, but lack of concentration is prevalent.

Their build does not appear particularly heavy or compact but radiates buoyancy and tension.

Posture, movement, motor skills

Posture

Already by their posture one can see the subconscious orientation as if something is constantly pulling or drawing them along. As is the case with Jesse, the upper body and head lean forwards and the shoulders are hunched and tense. The eyes, nose or chin, and sometimes all three, tend to jut out.

Also when seated their posture tends to be directed forwards, alert and hardly ever at peace. Their position when asleep can be rather convoluted. Their bed will be a mess and they tend to lie in the most impossible positions.

Movement

In their movement pattern you can recognize this being 'pulled along' by something. It is as if something moves them while they themselves are absent. A force seems to be at work that they are not able to master, demonstrated by their uncontrolled movements that have already finished before they have even noticed them. They tend to walk on tiptoes and skip, or run with large, bouncy steps, while their arms and legs, hands and feet are moving along.

If they have to sit still, their legs, feet and fingers will keep moving. They may fidget in their chair with their arms and legs all over the place. Many people with this constitution display tics, which can alternate rather quickly. Bobbie, for instance, does not only fidget in his chair, but also collects an unbelievable amount of little things in his pockets and other places. These will always appear at the wrong time, either falling down, breaking or flying through the air.

> Bastian (age 10, learning disability, TIQ 20, ASD), who calls himself, quite appropriately, 'the grasshopper', can only speak a few words. He prefers to hop about outside with his long thin legs, while all the time making grasshopper noises which he continues once inside, sometimes squeaking or humming.

This 'not being quite with it' may be observed when an object they are holding in their hands 'suddenly' breaks. Their hands did this without them noticing and they themselves are shocked by the result.

During the night, too, they are constantly moving and restless. A little boy was found crawling around his cot in his sleep. Sometimes even the head and the eyes do not stop moving. Here there is neither orientation nor dreaminess, only movement.

A stereotypical movement that often occurs is 'flapping', a kind of wing-like movement with the arms, sometimes accompanied by little hops. This happens out of excitement.

Motor skills

As may be understood from the above, they have poor motor functions due to tension, single-mindedness and poor control. Some adults and children with this constitution can get quite far with agility and endurance, but will then often have problems with precision or perseverance. They are good at running, climbing etc., but will usually have difficulties with gymnastics, cycling, swimming, roller-skating and other such activities, especially at first.

They have poor coordination and concentration. They can become confused and may react impulsively. When things go wrong they will start again, even though their body does not always want to cooperate. They will often fall, bump into things, have collisions or other accidents. These things just 'happen' and they don't know how!

Fine motor skills provide quite a stumbling block to them. Due to their urge to move they may not manage to make a pen, scissors or a knife function the way they want them to. They will squeeze their fingers tightly around them, so their hands become sweaty, the ink will smudge and go over the lines, or the knitting will become too tight making them feel powerless.

> Bobbie (age 13, learning disability, TIQ 60, ADHD and attachment disorder) thinks it would be great to make a wooden bowl with a chisel and a hammer. A teaching assistant is with him all the time to help him direct the chisel. The pieces are flying around, the work is progressing and Bobbie beams with joy. Then, in spite of all the precautions, the chisel goes right through the bottom. Bobbie looks disappointed, but very soon he wants to start again. He is hampered by his hurry to get everything finished quickly and by being diverted easily. Yet he really wants to make something.

They can sit quite still in front of the TV or the computer and almost seem to be creeping right into the appliance, unable to free themselves from it. Afterwards their restlessness will be even greater. When watching a play or a puppet-show you may see them sitting completely at peace, open-mouthed and wide-eyed. Here they are watching real movements and afterwards they will not be as restless.

Life processes

Digestive problems are common in people with this constitution: they may suffer from a sore stomach, diarrhoea and vomiting. They may eat little or much too fast, have many dislikes and find it hard to stay on their chair. They often dislike hot food, raw food and brown bread. Their digestion is poor (often right from birth) and they do not gain much weight. Many people are hyper-sensitive to sugar, colourings, taste enhancers and various other foods. They will react to these with increased agitation.

They often have poor body awareness and will feel little or no pain, coldness or tiredness. They do not notice what they are wearing. Sometimes their clothes look messy, even when brand-new. They will not tie their shoelaces and dislike having to wear a hat. They would prefer to always wear the same sweater or trousers.

Heart palpitations may occur. These may be caused by the fact that the life processes are too fast, but this has not been proven. The breathing is shallow and the voice often high-pitched. They usually fall asleep late and wake up early and then have problems staying in bed. Often this will already have been the case in infancy.

At night they sometimes suffer from nightmares and phobias and will then repeatedly get out of bed. People who have no boundaries often mature sexually at an early age, and will have endless energy. In those with poor body awareness sexual development may occur late. After the onset of puberty their restlessness will often diminish somewhat.

Behaviour

Thinking and perception

People showing characteristics of this constitution type often have a good capacity for thinking and are keen observers. They do, however, lack the inner peace to organize their thoughts, be more objective and see connections. The more active mental functions, such as that of associating and of making something concrete, will often develop, but there is a lack of thinking things through in advance or digesting experiences. They tend not to grasp puns or jokes, because they take everything literally.

> Anne (age 14, Mental Health Care, TIQ 90, ADHD and attachment disorder) was weaving with thick wool on a large wooden loom. All went well and the task was not too difficult for her. She was allowed to choose a new colour whenever one was finished. When the teacher came to have a look and said: 'Well, I have the feeling that blue and green are clashing', Anne put her ear to the loom and said: 'It's fine, I don't hear anything.'

They will hear and see everything but be unable to be objective or shut out impressions. They cannot screen anything out and will see whatever appears in their view. Each impression will lead to yet another impulse to move without any intervention of judgement or direction. They look, but do not see. They hear, but do not listen.[24]

They are unable to visualize the things they have experienced and will therefore hardly learn anything from them. This inability to visualize also means that they are unable to understand how other people experience things. This can be observed when they act in a play. They find it very hard to imagine themselves in someone else's position.

They do not have any time to really take in impressions and may talk incessantly, while reacting verbally to everything.

Their power of concentration is poor to very poor. They are exposed to impulses that are being called up by impressions. All this makes learning, both at home and in school, difficult for them as well as for their environment.

Some have such a strong urge to move and such limited conscious connection to their body and their environment, that speech development does not occur or is severely delayed. They may be diagnosed with ASD if this is the case, but those who do have speech are generally diagnosed with ADHD.

Feeling

Someone with characteristics of the 'too light' constitution will mostly feel overwhelmed. The other predominant emotion is single-mindedness caused by overstimulation. There is an inner turbulence, but an inability to explain why. There is usually no time to become aware of the (many and intense) emotions.

When it is quiet around them they appear to be very sensitive, able to have a delicate sense for things and sometimes also an ability to express this in words. They seem quite precocious, especially where they themselves are concerned, for instance in relation to moods and atmospheric changes. They have perfect hearing and are very perceptive. They appear to be very interested and socially aware.

At other times silence may frighten them due to the emptiness they feel when there are no longer any stimuli. They may then feel the urge to find diversion in the form of, sometimes extreme, stimuli like sweets, destruction or provocation. They really have a great need for order, for selective sense impressions and for someone who can bring clarity into their chaos. Changes and transitions will always bring back the fear of chaos and make them irritable.

Those with this constitution are essentially helpful and friendly and will go out of their way to do things for you. They are always happy to see you. Like those with 'too heavy' characteristics, they are trusting and open. The lack of harmony is not based in the emotional life, but the reactions from those around them do often make them feel inadequate. They fail, are punished, feel the anger from their environment coming towards them and do not know why. Is this really their fault!? They will then feel unstable and increasingly insecure. Sometimes they create a kind of bravura and pretend to be a tough dare-devil in spite of being faint-hearted, or they will make a fool of themselves.

If the urge to move is suddenly thwarted, someone with this constitution might react with fury or aggression and hurt others. They also have a tendency to escape or run away. Their social contacts are often superficial, although deeper contacts may come about occasionally. They often have too little inner peace for this and are too insecure and anxious.

> Bob (age 9, learning disability, TIQ 60, ADHD) has a housemate called Dave (forgetful). They are inseparable. Bob is always active and will talk to Dave incessantly. He will also always go ahead when they are roaming through the bushes. When Bob wants to break off a thick branch, Dave looks on. He is quiet and accommodating and keeps saying: 'Yes', while laughing a little.
>
> Then Bob, full of bravery, will say: 'Come on, then', and there they go again, pushing or breaking something (that was already broken) or tidy it up. They are truly inseparable.

At times, some, but not all, people with this constitution may play quite nicely with younger children, but they would need someone to keep an eye on them. Some might find a person in their surroundings in whom they can confide, such as a shopkeeper or a handyman. At a later age they will usually try and find someone, even those without speech.

Doing

People who show these characteristics always seem to be busy, although they may not really be 'doing' anything. They are all action, and will, for instance, have already taken the lids off all the dishes before anybody is even seated at the table. They will have poured your tea before they see where your cup is, and will have put sugar into it before they hear you say whether you want it or not. They mean well and are very helpful. They may start something, be it a game or setting up a mini-railway, but will not complete it (unless it is quiet around them), or they may lose bits and will then move on to the next thing. Many, like Bob, enjoy being outside. They are easily tempted into mischief and exciting adventures such as lighting a fire, stealing or being a nuisance. Something always happens and they see no danger. They like to tell others what they should do and what is allowed and what is not. Some people in whom this constitution is more pronounced can be completely absorbed in one play-thing, be it a little stick or a piece of string which they will twiddle constantly.

During puberty they can become quite unreasonable and run away at any attempt by their educators to start a conversation or make an arrangement.

> Steven (15 years old, Mental Health Care, TIQ 60, ADHD) wanted to go to cookery school and to everyone's delight he was accepted. He lived in a 'supported living' situation. Every morning he would leave on time with his packed lunch and get on a bus. After three months, the school phoned the support worker to say that he had only been seen at school for a day and a half and after that no longer. He explained that he had been wandering around on all the other days.

At this stage in life sexuality can begin to play a large part, sometimes in the form of extreme masturbation, sometimes in the form of a strong urge for sexual satisfaction. It is not unusual for girls in their vicinity to become their victims.

People with this constitution may look for provocation and excitement, take risks and sometimes go too far and will then become destructive, steal and show aggression. Their thirst for action could turn into a kind of addiction, unless boundaries are set for them.

In young people this feeling of tension which they want to get rid of may lead, at an early age, to smoking, drinking, experimenting with drugs and an increased risk of criminality. Their behaviour may arouse much irritation, aggression and feelings of powerlessness in their parents and support workers. Sometimes they become the black sheep in the family and may be abused due to the family's powerless frustration, which will only increase their restlessness and challenging behaviour. As long as they are supported with understanding and firm guidance, it may be possible for them to learn an actual trade according to their abilities and, to their delight, be of service to others.

Interpretation

People with this constitution are usually diagnosed with ADHD and sometimes also with ASD or ODD (Oppositional Defiant Disorder). A large number of children and adults with attachment disorders or trauma are also diagnosed with ADHD. 'Balans', the Dutch centre for ADHD, drew up the following list of symptoms:

— attention deficit and concentration problems or
— hyperactivity or
— impulsivity or
— problems with the executive (organizational) functions.

The different types have not been described separately in this chapter.

Many people who show characteristics of the 'too open' and of the 'too forgetful' constitution as described in the previous chapters are also diagnosed with ADHD. Seen from the point of view of special education out of anthroposophy this description is not accurate enough. Restlessness occurs in any of the constitution types with an extroverted tendency, but it will show up every time in a different form and with a different background, calling for different approaches.

Compared to those with the 'too heavy' constitution whose movement, starting from the metabolic system, is too *slow,* the movement of those who are 'too light' is too *fast.* Already in infancy they are usually too awake, will listen and look with intensity and have strong reactions and impulsive movements. They are less able than other infants to enjoy the feeling of contented satisfaction after meals. They often suffer from stomach cramps. Food is digested rapidly and does not allow them to gain much weight. There are thousands of metabolic disorders that have not yet been described scientifically. Children and adults with this constitution suffer from metabolic processes that are too fast and too superficial. This is why the brain (with its various synapses) has not developed fully, causing the symptoms mentioned above. In our time it is becoming ever more obvious that there is a connection with nutrition (see also below under 'Supportive approach'). Any stimuli will immediately result in quite strong impulses in the arms and the legs that simply *have* to be obeyed. One can see in children and adults who have improved control of their impulses that their intelligence and feeling may be intact but will soon be *overruled* by the impulse to move when they are stimulated.

On a [now defunct, tr.] website (Hersenstorm.com) we read the following: 'In cases of ADHD, PET [positron emission tomography, tr] scans show clearly the regions in the brain that do not function properly: the orbital frontal lobe of the large brain, right above the eyes, and in the "nucleus caudatus", deep in the centre of the brain. This may contribute to an aggravation of the learning disability.'

The frontal lobe of the brain functions as a basis for planning, overview and grasping greater connections. It is exactly these qualities that normally make people excel.

Keen observers may be able to detect in these people fluctuations of consciousness, causing their attention span and concentration to vary. This is usually most obvious in their ability to listen, which is sometimes very good, and at other times not so good at all.

Based on the idea that whatever takes place in the metabolic- and limb system is reflected in the brain, one may conclude that by treating the metabolism the brain function may also improve eventually. This has been proven recently (see also below in 'Supportive approach').

In many children with these characteristics the hyper-activity will decrease around the fourteenth year. Seen from the point of view of developmental psychology one could say that the child's own personality has begun to manifest within and that awareness of their own body is increasing. It may be the case that they are therefore better able to observe themselves and feel less exposed to impulses caused by stimuli.

Causes

Prenatal causes

In pregnancy:

- Infections, German measles, severe flu, virus.
- Drugs, use of alcohol.
- Hereditary factors (70%), metabolic disorders.

Often in boys:

- Difficult birth, prolonged labour.
- Umbilical cord around the neck, lack of oxygen.

Postnatal causes

— Accident, encephalitis (sometimes as a consequence of inoculations).
— Intolerance to food colourings, sugar (in children with B(asic) A(ttachment) S(yndrome) or to other foods; measles, whooping cough or mumps.
— Basic neglect before the seventh year.
— Trauma.

Supportive approach

Motto: setting boundaries.
Deep fear: continuous movement.
Greatest longing: peace, boundaries and predictability.

First of all try to calm down movements, then set boundaries and encourage awareness. Reward positive behaviour, ignore negative behaviour or try to tone it down. The attitude of the support workers must be extremely consistent and loving. Stop, think, and act.

From the above, it may be understandable that the 'pep-pill' Ritalin is often quite helpful here. A medicine for hyperactivity works because, due to the effect it has on the brain, it helps to really wake people up, in the sense of 'becoming aware'. (Ritalin may cause psychotic reactions in people who are 'too open'.) They finally have the possibility to see what they are doing and to begin to direct their actions. They learn to follow up their actions step by step with concentration and to think before they act. A consistent, clear approach and a very orderly structure will enable them to begin to experience themselves. The brake (i.e. consciousness) will then be provided by the support workers and not by Ritalin. After a long period of such support a person with the 'too light' characteristics will be able to experience him/herself right into the physical.

One of the most effective approaches for such a person is in the form of the 'little house'. This is symbolic for the friendly but firm boundaries that may be implemented in various ways—never as a punishment, but always as a preventative measure. It is advisable to find out which factors cause the person to be agitated. It is of no use to ask them something or to call on them once they are engaged in intense activity, because they will simply not hear you. The only useful thing to do is to join in with their movement so they notice you and then to try and make contact again.

Peter (age 36, learning disability, TIQ 20, ASD) will often hit his head with his hands and injure himself. When he is offered wristbands he will take them willingly and will ask for them whenever his inner agitation has increased due to too many impressions.

Timothy (age 17, learning disability, TIQ 20, ASD) always wears a harness that is held by someone when going outside. Without this he will run off unwittingly.

The 'little house' can be used literally: there may be a little wooden playhouse in the living room or common room. The child 'is allowed to' go in there and play (preferably at fixed times) before being overloaded by stimuli through visits or other events. Leaving them alone would cause anxiety. The important thing is the reduction of stimuli. They need something to focus their attention on, such as play or homework, something they can manage. If they get bored they will get restless and will look for action that is often unsuitable.

In cases of extreme restlessness (on doctor's advice) a child could be swaddled. This is a practice of wrapping up the child partly or completely for some time (as used to be done in the old days with babies in order to stimulate brain development.) Also a child's highchair could be used to provide the necessary boundary. Young children from one and a half to three years are usually 'too light'. This belongs to child development.

The idea of the 'little house' could consist of a series of clear arrangements in relation to activities, tasks and quiet moments that recur daily with strict regularity. It can also be used with adolescents and adults, as long as they understand the reason for it. It should be clear to them what they are allowed to do. Every time they succeed they will explicitly receive a confirmation or reward. This will stimulate their awareness. Things that go wrong will be ignored. One could use a reward system but this is rarely necessary. The principle of the 'little house' may also be found in the popular motto: *stop—think—act*.

Also in the care for the environment the principle of the 'little house' may be applied:

— Everything must be intact; what is broken will be removed immediately or repaired with the help of the person in question.
— Stimuli (colours, pictures, sounds and other impressions) should be gentle, limited and simple.
— Giving one's full attention to the person once or several times a day at fixed times is also a kind of 'little house'.

The 'little house' can be effective in various ways but should not be too big or too open, nor too small (like a prison). It must always be used as a preventative measure.

— The person wakes up because boundaries are visible.
— They will begin to develop rhythms and habits (giving structure to the etheric body), which has a long-term healing effect.
— They have an overview of the situation and know what to expect.
— There is no need for punishment or irritation, because less is going wrong.
— They cannot be blamed if the 'little house' is not applied properly.

Nutrition, clothing

— Food should not be spicy and not too solid (white flour and potatoes), but varied. Give them nourishing food that is easily digestible. Child psychiatrist Jan Buitelaar said: 'Children with ADHD usually respond positively to a strict diet. After a period of five weeks with the right food, seventy percent do not any longer show the criteria for the diagnosis; also oppositional behaviour decreases significantly.' He calls the results 'promising': 'The *Restricted Elimination Diet (RED)* is a hypoallergenic diet, adapted to the individual. Any foods that could provoke reactions in children, such as dairy, eggs, wheat, tomatoes and oranges, are left out over a period of five weeks. One is left with a strict elimination diet, usually consisting of rice, white meat, several types of fruit and vegetables and water. In this way it is possible to determine whether particular foods affect the behaviour of a child with ADHD. If this is the case, foods are reintroduced into the diet one by one. Then it will become clear to which specific food an individual child reacts.'[25]
— Camomile tea and, in the evening, a camomile compress on the stomach for a calming effect.
— The sleeping rhythm is often disturbed: try and limit impressions and promote relaxation after the evening meal.
— Provide them with sturdy, warm, tight-fitting clothing and shoes without wild colours or prints. Wool is too itchy. Soft cotton and silk are advisable while synthetic fabrics are not.

Activities, play

— Just like anyone else, those who are 'too light' need movement, as long as it is within limits.
— If something has gone wrong, it is good practice to go over the sequence of events with them step by step. Describe exactly what happened directly

before, during and after the event, where it could have been stopped (this is the task of the support worker), what were the consequences and who had not wanted what to happen. In this way you will come full circle and everything will be connected again (which is also like 'a little house'). This will then be remembered.

— People with this constitution like to *be active* and to *help*. It will have a positive effect to guide them in a consistent way as described above and to tune in with the person in such a way that *nothing* will go wrong. Take up a new activity before they become restless. Provide a space with a low level of stimulation.

— The imitation phase in early infancy is often missed out partly or completely. With children one can catch up on this through simple exercises, in which one lets them imitate movements, a way of walking or other actions in an exaggerated way. This will enhance wakefulness and awareness of their own movement. Doing this in a rhythmical, repetitive way, possibly with singing or a short verse, will have a more lasting impact.

— Structure and peace can be brought about by means of all kinds of children's games, such as ball games, playing shop, happy families etc. A nice way of setting boundaries and helping alertness could be via activities like treasure hunts with set tasks, relay-races, playing hide-and-seek etc, as long as the rules and instructions are clear and simple. As was explained above, adolescents and adults should be presented with structure and guidance in training and work.

— When watching television and using a computer they can sit still, but afterwards they will become restless.

— Images that can be internalized, as in stories, drama or a puppet show, will give the person more lasting relaxation. Images that belong together, as in the *Grimm's Fairy Tales,* may contribute to an inner structure that they lack so much. For adolescents and adults suitable literature should be found.

Supportive measures

– *Nutrition*
A diet plan by a dietician according to the elimination method.

– *Medication*
Anthroposophic medication can improve the metabolic processes and the self-regulating and formative functions. For general use: Aurum/Stibium/ Hyoscyamus, Organum quadruplex ampules, Hypophysis D6 and Cardiodoron.

The medicinal drugs Ritalin and Strattera are pep pills and can give clarity, but as soon as the medication has worn off there will usually be even more restlessness. The long-term effects are not known.

— External therapy
This therapy can also provide appropriate protection and warmth, enabling the organism itself to take control. Oil applications, baths and compresses can be of great help to experience one's own body. Swaddling is sometimes used so as to limit the excessive urge to move, shifting the emphasis to developing awareness in the head and the senses. Camphor oil may be applied to the legs.

— Physiotherapy
Also this is an excellent way to work on learning to move more consciously. Orientation exercises done at an accelerating pace with the hands, feet, legs and arms can be helpful.

— Healing environment
Restful pastel colours, such as pale green. Create an interior that to us seems bare without any unnecessary objects. Avoid broken things and only provide sturdy, unbreakable objects. Screen off an area.

— Eurythmy therapy
Working consciously with movement and learning to pay attention to it is important as a therapeutic approach. Rudolf Steiner indicated the sound sequence M, N, B, P, A (ah), U (oo). The sounds in eurythmy as a basis for movement have a direct relationship to the laws of movement of the etheric body, which is why they can work in a healing way.

— Art therapy
Most people with this constitution can achieve more when individually guided, rather than in a group. In various ways art therapy can increase wakefulness and the ability to direct and give form to things by oneself. Create forms with boundaries. Provide a quiet environment with few sense impressions.

— Music therapy
Music is based on very clear and objective laws. Listening and movement exercises are effective. Some people can manage to learn to play

an instrument which will not only have a therapeutic effect but will also boost confidence.

— Play therapy and conversation therapy.
Play therapy is probably only useful with firm guidance: leaving the child to his/her own impulses can lead to chaos and more anxiety. One can give form to feelings of failure, restlessness, urges etc, by working in a purposeful way with certain forms of play.

— Anthroposophic speech formation and mainstream speech therapy
Speech is really a subtle form of movement. Fast, impulsive and unformed speech can be improved by this approach.

— Cognitive behaviour therapy
This can help improve self-knowledge in children and adults with an IQ above 50 and from age10 upwards.

— Family therapy and family support
Educating someone with this constitution can be a challenge. Parents will usually first need family therapy and then support in daily life.

9
How Does it Feel?

The following is a description of how someone with a particular constitution might feel. These descriptions are based on the method of 'empathic observation' as was used with participants in workshops and with other people. This is how it can be done:

You try and feel if you have any new sensations when imitating for yourself one of the main characteristics of a constitutional type (such as having a very thin skin). Human beings really carry all human possibilities within themselves (and therefore also any of the constitution types), even though they only use a fraction of them. After having worked with this type of empathy exercises for a long time I have gradually begun to realize that trying to feel how it is to be someone else is not the point. The point is rather to widen one's own possibilities of perception. I have come to the conclusion that when following the instructions for practising 'empathic observation' one crosses the boundary of everyday human experience. When imitating the constitution of a person who is 'too open', for instance, one is able to consciously experience and describe this constitution within oneself. The more one practises this, the clearer the experiences will be.

Too compulsive: how does it feel?

I feel locked up as if behind a glass wall. I would like to make contact. I am longing for it. I am very sad because I do not manage. If only someone would understand. They will think that I am stupid or crazy. I am ashamed. It makes me happy when people understand and acknowledge me. I enjoy being with children or adults who are just like me. We already know each other a bit, can tolerate each other and have fun together. Then I am sometimes able to laugh.

I hardly feel my body and do not feel my legs at all. My head feels huge and full, too full. There are so many things inside it buzzing around. I can't get rid of them and they give me headaches. This makes me angry. Where can I put it all?

I am afraid that it is accumulating and I will not be able to bear it any longer. I am worried that my head will explode.

I will now go up and down in the lift once more (obsession with elevators) and hope these feelings will stop.

If things happen differently from how I imagined them I panic because then it is all wrong. Sometimes I get into such a panic that I smash up everything or I will pick up something and throw it. People move things and then I have to put them back again in the right place.

There is no space. Don't make such a noise!

If only everything could stay the same. Otherwise I will just have to touch it. I want coffee!

Sometimes we get food that is all mixed up. How can they come up with such a thing!

Maybe that is why I am constipated! I would like to be able to cry.

What I am good at, though, is making beautiful things and people admire me for that. Exact drawings, pottery tea sets; I can engrave glass, play music etc.

Too forgetful: how does it feel?

I feel happy. I enjoy jokes and making people enthusiastic. I like playing and planning things. Maybe I will make something or join a campaign for Greenpeace.

I don't know what people want from me. I feel empty, restless. I want to do something.... I cannot remember that word. Why don't I remember things? They told me to do something but I have forgotten what, so I just do what comes into my head. The same happens at school.

I want to live on my own like the others. Why am I not allowed to? I don't understand why they get cross with me. I am so ashamed when I cannot remember something. I try to think up little tricks so no one will notice.

They asked me what I would like to have and I said: 'A new memory.'

I love listening to music, singing, playing an instrument. I still know all the songs I have learned!

I want things to stay where they are. I am happy in my own room. I love an open fire or a candle or a campfire. I also love water, especially with lots of foam.

They asked me to draw a firebird and I did. Then they said that it was a little chick. I love yellow. What should I draw then?

I need something to make me normal, but I don't know what. I hope someone will come who knows.

Too congested: how does it feel?

I often feel really unwell. Then I cannot get going. They ask me things and call me, but it doesn't work. I am stuck. There is something inside that makes me anxious. It presses and pushes from within. It makes me feel nervous. I want it to go away.

I usually stay with the adults, so nothing will go wrong.

I feel it all the time. I cannot hear or see you very well. The thing inside me is too strong. Maybe it will go away when I move a bit; such tension! I cannot stand it anymore. Please, do something. Stupid people!

Sometimes that feeling is not there. Then I feel so well and light and I can do so much more. I wish it would stay like that way for ever. This is really me.

I am getting furious, it is rising up inside me. I have to do something! I scratch my little sister; much too hard! That is not good! I throw a table over. It helps for a moment.

It is rising even higher than a fireball. I don't know anymore where I am and I am falling … and when I finally wake up, I feel so exhausted that I am going to have a long sleep.

I think everybody is stupid because I have to feel this bad. Those doctors don't really know anything. I don't want these people around me; shit! Everything feels dark.

Too open: how does it feel?

I so badly want the world to be beautiful, with lovely colours and nice music. Then I feel well. I want to draw and write stories; I know I can do that. But if they don't give me any peace I cannot do it. I love acting in a play and being a princess and then I will tell all the others what they have to do. Then it will be a very nice play and everybody will come to watch it. And I will be the star.

Ouch, all that noise! It is coming from all sides. All these children, doing all kinds of things. Ouch, I cannot stand it. It hurts. I am scared. It all goes right into me. I cannot protect myself. They have to stop, don't they know that? I am just going to go to that little one over there, because his screaming irritates me. I am sending him out. Why doesn't my mother do anything about it? She is a weakling!

The whole day long things are happening that I cannot cope with. I want to stay in bed with my head under a blanket. They won't do anything about it anyway. Nobody knows how bad it is. The world is so stupid! Everybody, except very young children and animals and sick people. Sometimes I keep tapping so I can feel that I have a body. Otherwise it is a 'nothing' with a voice. Full on the outside and empty inside. I feel tension in my whole body.

The adults have to help me. I will make sure they will. I'll stay with them. There is no one else to turn to. When they also begin to talk loudly, I will be even more anxious. Then I want to go away. I am afraid I will fall to pieces. They have to help me. I cannot do it!

Too heavy: how does it feel?

I am happy with my life. I don't like getting up early in the morning. I enjoy being with lots of people. They should not tease me, because that makes me ill. I also like school, but it is too difficult. I cannot finish my work. Don't tell anyone. Then I will get cross. It is quite nice here; I love baking bread.

Yesterday we had a party with music, André Hazes [a popular Dutch singer, tr.]; he is good, isn't he? I danced with Jane. I was allowed to play the piano. Did you see my parents? They were there too. And my sister and my cousin. It was my cousin's birthday and we had a big cake; it was delicious! I like being with you.

Later on I want to get married and live together with Jane, so nice! I also want to work in the bakery and make coffee. Then watch television and have early nights. Nobody is allowed to interfere.

People do have to come and pick me up, otherwise I will stay in my chair for hours. An outing in the car! Walking is good. I want to do it more often but I cannot manage.

I don't know what's the matter with me, but I just can't go any faster. Do you not understand? My body is heavy and I cannot help it. Please, have a little patience and then I will happily do what you want from me.

Too light: how does it feel?

I really don't want to fidget and move so much, but I just cannot stop myself. This little motor keeps running on. I'll be taking off if nobody holds me down. I am dragged along by it, it's taking over. Then I am unable to sit still. Then I just keep pottering around or drink something to calm myself down. I'll tease someone who is weaker than me, or do something funny, or get into mischief with others.

I need someone or something to stop me. I am afraid that this little motor is getting ever stronger. Maybe someone who is stronger and more peaceful than this little motor can help me. Otherwise I will not manage to keep myself quietly occupied. I want it so very badly. I can see other people do it. I also want to be able to do lots of things.

I feel overwhelmed. There is too much mess here and too much commotion.

Sometimes I am calm, like recently with the lady in that room with almost nothing in it.

She was good at it. I liked her and I was able to do lots of sums. I know I can do it! If only it could be quiet and empty…

Later I want to work with other people. It looks like fun. A good job, where I'll know exactly what to do. I can work hard. It will be alright. I'll just start over again every time.

The constitution types in drawings

On the following pages, drawings have been included by children with a learning disability and/or challenging behaviour. With the exception of the first drawing, these drawings have been arranged in pairs of opposite constitution types.

The last three drawings were done by a child with a history of trauma.

In theories about children's drawings there is a general assumption that children draw a house and the human body the way they experience their own bodies.

These drawings were selected because certain aspects of a constitution type are recognizable in them, besides the personal characteristics of that child at that moment.

Picture 1: A 16-year-old boy, ASD with compulsive behaviour, TIQ 60. Thin, straight lines, as realistic as possible with exact details. Someone with the tendency to obsessive behaviour usually likes to draw this way. The fact that some walls and floors in this drawing are collapsing is not typical.

Picture 2: A 10-year-old boy, ASD with compulsive behaviour, TIQ 40. Densely coloured square shapes and a dark, threatening sky are characteristic for this constitution type. The doors are shut and there is no one else to be seen. Strong pressure was used on the pencil. In drawings by a person with this constitution colours are usually absent or rather sombre and the angles are quite severe.

Picture 3: A 10-year-old girl, PDD-NOSD, TIQ 50, forgetful. The house has a childlike, roundish shape and is transparent. The drawing appears light and cheerful with decorations all over. Birds are dancing and there are flowers in the sky. There are two smaller buildings on either side supporting the house that leans over against a rather airy background. The doors and windows are blocked up. These elements correspond with the constitution.

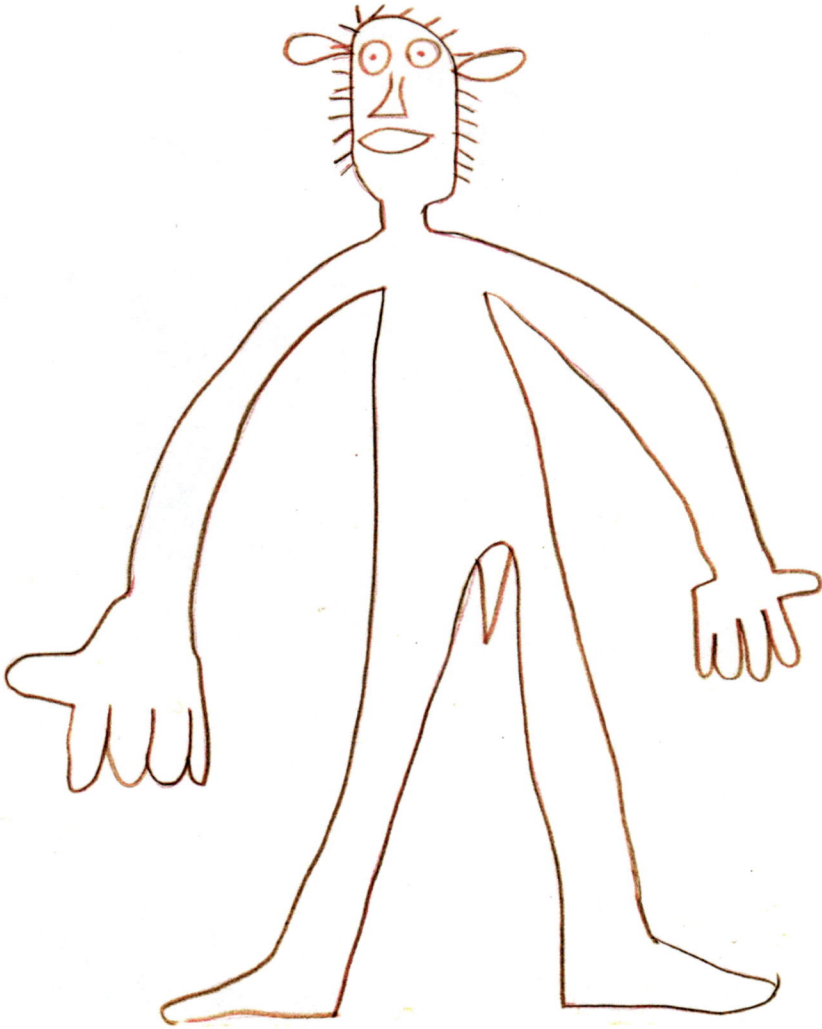

Picture 4: An 11-year-old boy, ASD with compulsive behaviour; TIQ 40. The man has been clearly drawn in one thin line. His sense organs—eyes, ears, nose and mouth—are clearly visible and therefore important. The eyes express fear and anger; the man's posture is threatening and tense. He is clearly aware of his hands, feet and penis. There is no background, no ground and there are no people. These characteristics are partly typical for this constitution type, although one does not usually see so much expression in the drawings.

Picture 5: A 12-year-old boy, ASD, forgetful, TIQ 30. It seems as if the man is ascending. His face is anxious and his hair is standing on end. Around him there are colours of fire and sulphur, red and yellow. And a little devil, too! There are buttons all down his body. Are they holes, or places where memories that refuse to come back up have got stuck? Little yellow balls (sulphur) are bubbling up next to him. Is he unable to place them? All elements belong to this constitution.

Picture 6: An 8-year-old boy, too congested, TIQ 60. The house in this drawing is very small and not coloured and there is only a tiny, closed door and a very tiny window. The thick many- coloured trails coming from the roof of the house are much more significant. Little demon faces are floating above the longest trail. You are forcefully pulled out of your house (your body) and that gives you an awful feeling. These elements belong to the constitutional type of being 'too congested' and are very typical for this child.

Picture 7: A 15-year-old girl, ASD, too open, TIQ 40. The house has windows/holes everywhere, the occupant is exposed to the surroundings and can see everything. The house, moreover, has some kind of antennae. There is a faint indication of sky. The colour is pale and has been drawn with hardly any pressure. Only one colour has been used. The house does, however, have a solid foundation. This is not always the case in drawings by this type of person.

Picture 8: A 6-year-old boy, epilepsy, TIQ 30. The figure in this drawing has hardly any head and no face. It seems that the thickly coloured patches on the body are dominant in the experience: a dense area, an organ-like shape and then another dense area below it. There is some kind of background, be it slightly vague. These elements, as well as others, occur more frequently in drawings by people with a 'too congested' constitution.

Picture 9: A 9-year-old girl, too open. She says about her drawing: 'A poor little girl. She only has tiny arms...walks on her feet...bare feet...I am poor...miserable. She has scratches on her feet and that is very bad for the child...she really needs crutches, otherwise she will not be able to walk.' The drawing is finely executed and well observed. She also says: 'Later, when I grow up, I might well become something that I do not want to be.' The little girl's arms reach out, asking for help. This way of drawing belongs to the 'too open' constitution type.

Picture 10: A 13-year-old boy, attachment disorder and ADD, too heavy, TIQ 50. This castle—or is it a church?—, stands very simply, solidly and compactly on the ground. The drawing is uncomplicated with large areas…The building has been placed at the bottom of the page and is nearby. These characteristics fit the constitution of being 'too heavy'. The fact that nothing can be seen inside the building and that the sunbeams are black could be connected with the attachment disorder.

Picture 11: An 8-year-old boy, attachment disorder and ADHD, too light, TIQ 65. The castle has been drawn very quickly and it does not appear very strong. We can see watchful men with swords and shields. The men have been drawn in a childish way and have no faces. There appears to be terrible fear of an enemy. A fortified escape route has been made to the strongest tower. The great fear of the enemy may be partly linked to the attachment disorder, while the other elements fit the constitution type of being 'too light'.

Picture 12: A 17-year-old girl, ADD, ASD, too heavy, TIQ 30. The drawing is simple in every aspect, and has been made with great care. This is visible from the careful, dense colouring. The woman in the picture appears rather heavy and immobile in spite of her cheerfully coloured clothing and hair. The sun is beautifully yellow and glows without any beams. The ground is solid and clear. We can find all these aspects in drawings by people with a constitution that is 'too heavy'.

Picture 13: A 9-year-old boy, attachment disorder and ADHD, too light, TIQ 65. In the background we can see two trees and a rickety house that has been drawn quickly and a little shakily. In the foreground we can see a little man with a bear's head; the man is not looking very happy, in spite of the yellow head. At the top of the page there is a UFO, as the boy called it. It looks rather compact. It is clear that the boy must have seen the little man and the UFO somewhere, forming the kind of impressions that have stayed with him to such a degree that its colour and clarity overpower his 'own' drawing. This occurs more often in children with a constitution that is 'too light'.

Picture 14: A 10-year-old boy, attachment disorder and trauma, TIQ 50. In the first drawing we can see two people against a very vague background. The person on the left is the doctor, the one on the right is the boy himself as an adult. The person on the right seems to be ejaculating and showing it to the doctor. He must be ill. The doctor is shocked and looks the other way.

Picture 15 is by the same boy as picture 14. The figure is on fire, burning with the emotions that are so strong that he is unable to control them. His eyes are closed and he pulls a face that is twisted in terrible pain. His body has not been coloured in, possibly due to a lack of emotions and being closed off.

Picture 16 is by the same boy (see 14 and 15). The solitary figure in this drawing is standing unsteadily on a flat area; his body is leaning forward and there are blotches (wounds or holes?) all over it. His face is twisted into a grimace. He seems powerless and unable to keep himself upright and deal with his body.

10
Attachment Disorder / Trauma

In this book I have chosen to mainly describe the anthroposophic extensions to the approach to this disorder. In the field of Learning Disability and Mental Health it often occurs in adults with learning disabilities and has a bearing on their constitution. The underlying constitution determines how a person reacts to a lack of attachment, to neglect or to abuse, (vulnerability theory). Children from the same family may react completely differently to neglect, even if it was the same for all of them. Sometimes one of the children will continue to live at home, while another child has to be admitted to an institution for quite some time.

People with an attachment disorder and trauma have here been described as part of the same group, but sometimes we will briefly refer to particular phenomena especially connected with physical and sexual abuse. We will not describe here the behavioural characteristics of these children and adults, (often diagnosed with borderline disorder or personality disorder). These are generally known and may be found elsewhere[26]. We will, however, describe the typical points for observation used in anthroposophic diagnosis. The anthroposophic approach could add something to the interpretation and treatment. Issues such as trauma, dissociation and sexual abuse have also been described in an excellent way by Annejet Rümke.[27]

The phenomena of stealing, lying and destructive behaviour will be described separately in this chapter from the specific point of view of anthroposophic remedial education.

Posture, movement, motor skills

Posture
It is striking that many children and adults who show characteristics of this disorder have tense, hunched up shoulders causing their chest to be somewhat retracted and their back visibly tense. The head seems to be slightly forward, giving the impression of someone always on the

alert. The hands are often bent tensely or clenched into fists. Some who always have their mouth open often also have a strongly protruding belly and certain habitual gestures like twisting a lock of hair, sucking their fingers etc, as occur in certain phases of early childhood development.

Movement

Legs and hands are usually moving and you can frequently see twitches near the eyes or mouth. The look is searching, anxious or blank. Typical for the movement pattern is not completely owning the movements. These are often uncontrolled, not flowing, but tense and jerky, be it sometimes only slightly yet clearly visible as movements.

Motor skills

The gross motor movements are often too forceful, misdirected or too slow. In the fine motor skills the person's tension and poor concentration tend to form a barrier. When writing or doing craftwork the hands are cramped. In knitting the thread is pulled too hard causing the knitting to become too tight and smudged, stitches to drop and the knitting to be pulled about. Cutting or gouging wood may go off target, or the movement may be too forceful.

In games of skill the control is poor and the tension too great. There is an inability to give sufficient direction to the movement.

A good observer will notice in posture, play and movement characteristics left over from early childhood. These elements might well point to the moment in time when disturbances occurred in an otherwise healthy development.

Life processes

Adults or children with an attachment disorder will usually feel uncomfortable in their body. This unpleasant feeling of tension often leads to restlessness, smoking, drugs and alcohol abuse, obesity and other problems. The skin colour is often greyish or pale, and pale brown in those with a dark skin. The lips are pale, the eyes sometimes red–rimmed.

People with these characteristics are sometimes thin or a little plump. Small wounds tend to heal slowly and are being scratched open continuously.

They often have complaints, such as tummy-aches, diarrhoea, constipation and headaches, as well as sleeping problems. If a child or adult
with an attachment problem is worried about something, this will often
manifest as a physical complaint. They easily catch a cold. They will either
gobble down their food and appear not to taste anything, or hardly eat
anything and be very choosy. Sometimes their growth is very slow.

They are easily tired and worried about things.

Interest in sexuality often develops early, long before the possibility
of any close relationship, while in others sexual development may be
delayed.

Their clothing is quickly grubby and torn, hanging out or messy.
Shoelaces are undone, buttons are missing, one sock may be lost and
stains tend to appear out of the blue.

They are often hyper-sensitive to minor ailments yet do not seem to
be bothered by cold, heat or illness.

Interpretation

If a child does not receive the right physical, emotional and sensory
nourishment, he/she will lack the basic elements for a healthy development of body and soul. Children will live in a continuous state of tension,
causing a permanent state of cramp (trauma), if they do not feel safe or
are being threatened and fear for their lives. The child will develop great
caution and alertness in order to survive. At this early age such skills are
developed at the expense of the life processes and will usually result in
permanent damage to the organs. They also tend to hamper the gradual
development of play, imagination, movement, the emotional life and the
ability to learn.

Fear dominates: the fear of not getting what you need, the fear of
encountering things you cannot cope with.

Someone with such problems does not experience the body as something to identify with, as it does not provide any foundation or safety.
This deficit, experienced as a hole, is a wound that does not heal. This
hole causes unpleasant sensations, dark negativity, a fear of falling apart,
suffocating anger and insatiable desires. These emotions will show up
their great vulnerability and will condition their behaviour.

Marilyn (age 12, TIQ 90, attachment disorder) loves animals and enjoys playing with little children, which she can do very nicely. As soon as she is on her own, strange things happen: suddenly a young animal lies dead, a little child has bruises on its arms.

Some people, especially those who were sexually or physically abused, tend to split off from their body (dissociation). They will then no longer, or only partially, experience their body as their own and this causes feelings which they find unbearable. Self-mutilation in order to avoid those feelings occurs frequently. At the same time they will develop an endless number of strategies in order to try and catch up on the protection and love they have been lacking.

Disturbances in the life processes may originate from food deprivation (on various levels), or from a threat. The challenging behaviour is the *consequence*. Neglect at a later age (7-14 years) will especially result in disturbances in morality and may cause depression and aggression. This can also be the case with people who experience severe trauma as an adult.

The physical consequences of attachment disorders, attachment problems and trauma are mirrored in the brain. From an anthroposophic point of view, the brain is seen as an organ that mainly synthesizes, mirroring everything that happens within the body.

Supportive approach

The idea that the individual core of a human being is always sound (see Chapter 1) is very relevant for people with a trauma. No matter how disturbed their behaviour may be, one should not lose sight of the fact that there is an individual inside who *does* want to develop, make contact and become well. It is *always* and in any situation possible to communicate with this aspect of the person. The awareness that behaviour is not what we *are* but what we *have* is of vital importance. This means that it should always be made clear that one may disapprove or approve of a certain type of behaviour, but *never* of the individual. The inner core has a spiritual origin and is always 'good'. If this insight is put into practice very consistently, significant improvement may be achieved.

Just as in diagnosing a particular illness, it is important to ascertain in which developmental stage the adult or child is (this has usually already been tested). One can see from the person's speech, thought patterns, social behaviour, play, movement and leisure activities, that there is emotional or intellectual delay (sometimes quite a sizable one) in some areas and not in others. It is important to pay attention to *both* levels, offering developmental opportunities on both levels rather than on only one. Should the latter happen the consequences could be disastrous, such as a serious relapse or severe forms of aggression.

> Mike (age 17 years, Mental Health Care, TIQ 90, PDD-NOS) was doing quite well in the everyday life of the institution and was independent in many respects. He had made good progress at a secondary school for special education. His support workers became very annoyed at his habit of popping up unexpectedly again and again calling out 'peekaboo'. They decided that he was not allowed to do this any longer. Three weeks later he threatened the teachers with a large knife that he had found in the school kitchen.

Mottos for the support-workers' approach:

— Make contact, but never expect anything!
— Ignore (verbal) aggression and do not get irritated.
— Be safe and predictable.
— Show respect and set a good example.
— Reward any achievement no matter how small.
— Never disapprove of the person, only of their behaviour. Try and 'label' positively.
— Do not expect too much.
— Praise their outer appearance frequently.
— Stand in solidarity with the parents.

The life processes should be restored and cared for as much as possible; the caring should be done ever more by the person themselves. This may be done by establishing a generally rhythmical, varied day programme with few stimuli, with the help of good food, play, movement, rest, a healing environment, learning activities and work.[28]

Initially, external therapies are the most effective, as they improve the basic physical functions. Then there are possibilities to improve disturbed behaviour and health by means of therapies that support coping strategies and build up mental health, such as play therapy, art therapy, music therapy, speech therapy, eurythmy therapy and anthroposophic medication.

The various therapies offer ways, via the life functions, to have a healing influence on the coping process and the excessive alertness. They can also diminish fear, irritability and shock, and improve sleep and concentration. These therapies are aimed at the individual and are different for each person depending on the condition of the four levels in the constitution (body, life processes, behaviour and individuality).

Talking about things and digesting them is also important, as is offering understanding, protection and security. Do not be secretive. Work on a sound basis and in partnership with them. Distraction through work and family. Do not identify with the person (by showing that you understand the reason for their behaviour).

Treatments aimed at trauma, such as EMDR (*Eye Movement Desensitization and Reprocessing*), can be used. The American child psychiatrists Bruce Perry & Maia Szalavitz describe in their book *The Boy who was Raised as a Dog* how brain research in children with severe trauma can point to the origin of the damage. In the 'Neuro-Sequential Model of Treatment' they describe a therapeutic cycle, that is remarkably similar to the methods based on anthroposophic ideas. This treatment brings about clear improvement, also in the brain.

Supportive attitude

Do not punish but be clear about what 'we' want and do not want. This also applies to stealing, lying, bullying and destructive behaviour.

Sending them out to the corridor or their room on their own can be too frightening (yet another rejection!) and could lead to increasingly demanding behaviour or to intransigence.

Correcting challenging behaviour would be ineffective, because it will be felt as being judged again—the person had already been 'deemed a failure'. There is already a question of very low self-esteem, so behaviour will not improve but confidence will diminish. A new type of behaviour can be demonstrated or offered. It is better to ignore disturbing behaviour and to reward positive behaviour, even in relation to the most matter-of-course and small things.

> In one of the groups the group leader would always ask the young teenagers with attachment problems how school had been for them. There were hardly any replies. Another group leader would start lunch in a different way. She would say: 'How nice to have lunch with you and it is great that you are all here.' And she meant it, too! Then they would spontaneously tell their stories.

When something has gone wrong it helps to set things right by means of positive action; words alone will not do. It is not necessary to ask for reasons. Contact will then be restored and may be confirmed.

Attention

It can be helpful to give extra love and attention at designated times, for instance by doing an activity together with the child or adult once or twice a day at the same time of the day and giving them your full attention, so they can begin to rely on it. Doing this consistently, for instance every day at a certain time or in a different clear rhythm, will enable them to build on it. This will boost their confidence. At other times of the day you could then say: 'Later on, when I really have time for you.' Their demanding behaviour may then decrease because there is less need for it. Then it might even be possible that they can play, read or rest in their room on their own, not as a punishment but by arrangement.

Setting an example

Because people with an attachment disorder or trauma have a strong sense of justice and imitation of others, support workers should set a good example in whatever they ask of them.

> A group leader of a group of adolescents with these problems was an expert at repairing bicycles and loved doing it. Very soon the group was running a bicycle repair shop in which others could have their broken bikes repaired.

By imitating others they will learn to show respect for and be considerate of other people and the environment, after which they will also be able to transfer this to themselves and their own environment at school or work. In this way they can be made co-responsible as appropriate to their age, as long as one does not count on it. When things do not work out so well it will help *to work together with them*. The more they accomplish, the greater their self-confidence will be.

> Walter (age 19, Mental Health Care, TIQ 80, OCD, attachment disorder) lived within the protective environment of an institution for a long time. His parents had split up and he visits his father regularly. As a young child he experienced traumatic events and neglect. He has a strong tendency to compulsions, has hardly any awareness of his body and never laughs or cries. It is very hard to get him moving. At 18 he wished to live with his father and this was made possible. In retrospect he seemed to have become so furious about some of his father's habits that he could not bear it any longer. In a fit of anger he seriously wounded his father.

Activities, play and work

When they are involved in activities it is good to challenge them to push their boundaries.

'Yes, you can!'

Finishing a product on their own or helping someone else will boost their confidence.

Stories, pictures, drama, religious rituals, celebrating festivals, nature, beautiful colours, music, sports etc. are a form of nourishment. People with an attachment disorder may show a lot of resistance against these things and one should not put any pressure on them, but use a matter-of-fact, persuasive approach. Stories, pictures etc. can give a certain satisfaction free from any relationship. These objective elements can provide the nourishment that was lacking. You can tell by the keen way these activities are being taken up that they are helpful to them.

Destructiveness, stealing, lying

Destructive behaviour, stealing and lying can be looked upon as behaviour that in a certain way (and under a different name) belongs to the healthy human being. In those with attachment disorders, however, this behaviour manifests in a distorted form. Destructive behaviour, stealing and lying are often a consequence of an attachment disorder.

Destructiveness

In everyday life we can exist, amongst other things, due to the fact that we destroy and break down. Our metabolic system makes sure that each bit of food is destroyed fully. This starts from the very moment that we put food into our mouth, add saliva to it and chew. Once eaten, no part of a carrot remains intact.

Destructive behaviour stems from a destructive aspect over which the person does not have any control. It can manifest in different ways:

— Quite unconsciously: as if in a dream any toy or book that gets into their hands will be destroyed as soon as there is a minute when their support workers are not around. Afterwards they themselves are shocked.
— Sometimes we may see that the destructiveness manifests together with nervousness, clumsiness or haste. It seems as if anything they pick up simply has to be dropped, torn or broken.
— In others it will manifest in a kind of pleasure, based on anger, in hurting others or themselves, or in a strongly compulsive way.

Destruction belongs to the metabolic system. In people with characteristics described here the digestive process has often been neglected from birth onwards. They usually also have digestive problems. It will therefore be exactly at this point that the treatment can begin. Punishment, losing one's temper or corrections are ineffective. Experience has shown that the disturbed behaviour may well begin to decrease as soon as there is improvement in the digestive processes.

Apart from this it has to be made clear to them that destructive behaviour cannot be tolerated. What is broken can be fixed or thrown away. It is important to always assume that things are not done on purpose.

Stealing

Everybody steals all day long in a way that we all judge to be legitimate. We are not aware that while we are listening to a friend, to a teacher or to the television, we continually take in ideas, thoughts, discoveries and methods, and make them our own. We do not call this stealing, but as soon as material objects are involved we do call it pinching or stealing.

An activity that is sound in the domain of the mind has been shifted to the hands. We expect of a child from the age of about four the ability to distinguish between these two activities; the one is allowed, the other one is not. There are also different forms of stealing:

— It can happen anywhere, visible to anyone and is usually rectified after a remark has been made about it.
— A person intentionally goes looking for someone's favourite things and 'knows' that this is not allowed. They will take things, hide them or give them away.
— The person knows exactly how to seek out money, jewellery and keys in such a crafty manner that no one (including themselves) understands it. No lock or storage space is safe (kleptomania).

This kind of behaviour in a child or adult tends to make us feel angry and powerless. Alertness has been transferred to the hands, although it belongs to the head, which in a person with these characteristics is very much awake, be it in a way that is rather one-sided and not connected to feeling and thinking. In early childhood insufficient challenges and nourishment have usually been given to their intellectual, cognitive side. This is where we must start to work if we want to help decrease the disruptive behaviour. This means giving plenty of 'nourishment' (stories, knowledge, special interests), waking up and alerting at their own level, and including feelings of wonder, enthusiasm and interest. This must be done in a non-coercive, playful manner and with humour. Punishment, anger or prohibition do not work here either, while prevention and making up do.

In eurythmy therapy one could work intensively on creating awareness of hands and feet by means of physical exercises (for instance with the sound 'E' ('ay').

Medication: sugar D6 injections, [homeopathic doses of] lead.

It can be helpful if they know that a particular person whom they trust is aware of their frequent behavioural difficulties and that this person disapproves of the behaviour rather than of them as a person. In spite of this type of behaviour they almost always realize what is right and when something was wrong.

Stealing may also occur if the lack of love and protection is experienced as an empty hole. Stealing remains an unsuccessful way of filling in the hole. As the emotional life is involved here, it is important to incorporate into the support structure more attention and a sense of security.

Lying

Our imagination is able to fit elements from life together in new combinations. We can imagine buying a beautiful car, making a lovely journey to a faraway country and meeting very special people over there. We can also do this in relation to our past: 'I wish I had not said that, then things would have turned out differently.'

If we are of sound mind we will know exactly where the *boundary* between imagination and reality lies, no matter how strongly we wish to make something come true. We are aware of the fact that all kinds of things have to be done to make this happen.

In lying, this boundary has shifted. Things are being experienced as real. Your wishes become reality and things you do not want to know have never happened.

The world of fantasy becomes a reality created by oneself:

— Sometimes things that have happened are quite subconsciously denied or ascribed to others (as in a small child).
— Others may present particular things they wish to be true as if they are established facts: 'My brother is a police officer.'
— Lying may also be used as a way to deny existing reality or memories.

This kind of behaviour occurs especially in adults and children who have not learned to live with unfulfilled wishes. Wishes were either never or always fulfilled.

Lying also occurs in people who have gone through experiences that burden their conscience in such a way (due to the fact that they were involved in them) that they are unable to bear them. It may also originate from feelings of uncertainty and mistrust. For instance, one thing might not have turned out as it usually has and suddenly 'the whole world is against me'.

Lying will not decrease if attention is drawn to it all the time. It is necessary to retain contact with reality on as many levels as possible; also absolute certainty whether or not they will get what they want, as well as the experience that it is possible to 'make up', be forgiven and repair what has gone wrong.

It is also important that they have someone nearby who they know is aware of the state of affairs; someone who helps them when telling how things actually happened and who will really listen without judging them for their behaviour.

In school, at work

It will often be necessary to let people with attachment problems and/or trauma participate in special education with smaller classes or in a smaller work setting.

A teacher or a work-coordinator may become a very important person in their lives, because the situation in a class or workshop is structured clearly, is predictable and safe and the teacher's or work-coordinator's role is not based on a personal relationship.

Apart from the pedagogical approaches mentioned earlier, it is in school and work of vital importance *never* to address them or give them tasks beyond their capacity, but only give them tasks that can affirm their abilities. Once self-confidence has been established they themselves will indicate if they want to do more. Their abilities may differ from day to day and you as support worker must not take them for granted.

It is important to reward every achievement.

Supportive measures

− *Medication*
For general use: Myrrh comp., Apis D6, Rosemary, Mel D6-D10. Foods that harmonize and are nourishing.

− *External therapies*
External therapies are usually necessary from the start in order to ameliorate the negativity and lack of trust in the relationship to the body. Nourishing baths, copper ointment rubbed into the feet, massage.

− *Physiotherapy*
To feel better in one's body and make it more agile. Relaxation. Fun, the joy of movement, martial arts.

– Eurythmy therapy
Protective and harmonizing movements and sounds. Beautiful gestures.

– Healing environment
A simple, clear interior design with sturdy materials and pale, clear colours. Immediately remove or repair anything that is broken. A room of their own with their own special belongings such as photographs, things from home, things they made themselves.

– Art therapy
Teach them what is beautiful and pleasant to look at. Discovering their own style; biography work, processing things.

– Music therapy
Learning to play and sing, choosing their own instrument and playing together with others. Let them compose their own song.

– Play therapy
Acting out fantasies and past events and expressing emotions as a form of processing things.

– Speech therapy
Processing through drama and puppet shows. Training in social skills and boosting of confidence. Acquiring social insight and social skills.

– Cognitive therapy and family therapy
Where appropriate.

11
Regular Syndromes and Constitution Types

Introduction

It is possible to recognize symptoms of the so-called regular syndromes in each of the six constitution types described above.

Attachment disorder and post-traumatic stress disorder will often reinforce the child's constitution. For instance, a sensitive child will become even more sensitive, a 'closed' child even more closed. The ability to process traumatic events is also determined by a person's constitution. At a later age one often comes across the diagnosis of 'borderline'.

The diagnosis of ADHD is given to children and adults as described in the chapter on the 'too light' constitution. Children who have restless movements and/or poor concentration may also have a 'too open' or 'too forgetful' constitution and are often diagnosed with ADHD too.

Children with Down's syndrome belong to those with a 'too heavy' constitution, although at a younger age they can be quite lively.

Psychotic behaviour, MCDD (Multiple Complex Developmental Disorder) or mood swings can be found in all constitution types, especially when the one-sided behaviour has become so extreme that alienating or more serious behavioural disorders begin to occur. Some inexplicable types of behaviour are described in the chapters on the constitution types.

Schizophrenia and psychosis are clinical pictures in which the balance between thinking, feeling and will has been disrupted to such a degree that alienation and bizarre behaviour begin to arise. There is no longer any grip on reality.

Depression more likely occurs in people with the 'too compulsive', 'too open' or 'too heavy' constitutions.

Diagram: the most well-known regular syndromes and the constitution types

too compulsive
obsessive compulsive
Asperger syndrome,
brain damage

too forgetful
Alzheimer / Korsakov

too congested
epilepsy
hypersensitivity

too open
fragile X syndrome

too heavy
ADD
Down's syndrome
Prader Willi syndrome

too light
ADHD

The following may occur in any constitution type:

— Autism.
— Autism spectrum disorder.
— PDD-NOS, OD, MCDD.
— Attachment problems, attachment disorder.
— Psychosis, borderline personality disorder, personality disorder.
— Schizophrenia (of which there are many types).
— Depression.

Symptoms of some regular disorders as described in the DSM- V (Diagnostic and Statistical Manual of Mental Disorders) mapped against particular constitution types

By placing the constitution types beside the symptoms of a regular clinical picture it becomes clear which of them could possibly be matched.

Possible symptoms of PDD-NOS now ASD (according to the journal *Balans*)

— Clumsy and anxious behaviour in social situations: *open, closed, compulsive, forgetful* constitution types.

— Poor understanding and use of non-verbal signals: *compulsive, closed, light* constitution types.

— Minimal or no learning from social experiences: *forgetful, closed, compulsive* constitution types.

— Lack of mutual contact with others: *compulsive* constitution type.

— Making a lonely and closed impression: *compulsive, closed,* (sometimes) *open* constitution types.

— Sticking fanatically to certain routines: *compulsive, open, heavy, forgetful* constitution types.

— Expressing themselves in a stubborn and quick-tempered manner (fear): *compulsive, heavy, open, forgetful, closed, light* constitution types.

— One-sided interests: *compulsive, open* (sometimes), *forgetful* (sometimes) constitution types.

— Developing rigid and compulsive behaviour patterns: *compulsive, open, closed* constitution types.

— Hypersensitivity to sensory stimuli: *compulsive, open, closed, light* constitution types.

— Limited sensitivity to sounds, images, temperature, touch: *closed* constitution type.

— Delayed language development: *heavy, closed, compulsive, forgetful* constitution types.

— Odd, old-fashioned use of language: *compulsive, open* constitution types.

— Always interpreting language literally: *compulsive, closed* constitution types.

— Clumsy, rigid movements: *compulsive, heavy* constitution types.

Schizophrenia / psychosis

Being somehow able to recognize less severe symptoms in the constitution types remains trial and error.[29]

Characteristic symptoms: two or more of the following, each present for the majority of the time over a period of one month (or less, if successfully treated):

1. Delusions: an *extremely open,* or a *closed* constitution type.
2. Hallucinations: an *extremely open, or a congested* constitution type.
3. Incoherent speech (e.g. frequently losing the thread or rambling): *extremely forgetful, light* constitution type.

4. Severely chaotic or catatonic behaviour: *extremely open, congested, heavy, compulsive* constitution type.
5. Negative symptoms i.e., dulled affection, poverty of thinking or of speech or apathy: *extremely forgetful, closed, compulsive, heavy* constitution type.

Social and occupational dysfunction

From the onset of the problem—and for a significant portion of the time—functioning will be significantly below the level previously achieved in one or more areas, such as work, relationships or self-care. It could be the case that if the onset took place in childhood or adolescence, the level expected in relationships, school or profession may not have been reached.

Duration: at least 6 months.

— Exclusion of schizoid-affective or mood disorders.
— Exclusion of substance abuse or somatic condition.
— Link with a P(ervasive)D(evelopmental)D(isorder).

If there is a history of ASD or PDD, schizophrenia will only be diagnosed if prominent delusions or hallucinations have been present for at least a month.

Reactive attachment disorder in infancy or early childhood

A) Markedly disturbed and developmentally inappropriate social bonds in most contexts, starting before the fifth year, as is visible from either (1) or (2):

1. Persistent failure to initiate or respond to most social interactions in a developmentally appropriate fashion, as manifested in excessive inhibitions (*too heavy, too compulsive, too open* constitution types), excessive vigilance (*too compulsive, too open, too light* constitution types) or highly ambivalent and contradictory responses, such as detachment, refusal, rigidity (*too open, too closed* constitution types).
2. Superficial attachments as manifested in indiscriminate sociability with a marked inability to exhibit appropriate selective attachments (*too forgetful, too light* constitution types).

B) The disturbance in criterion A cannot be solely explained as originating in a developmental delay (as in learning disabilities) and does not meet the criteria of PDD.

C) Pathogenic care as evidenced by at least one of the following:

1. Persistent disregard for the child's basic emotional needs for consolation, encouragement and affection.
2. Persistent disregard for the child's basic physical needs.
3. Repeated turnover of primary care-staff, preventing stable attachments being formed.

D) There is reason to assume that the type of care in criterion C is the cause of the disturbed behaviour in criterion A.

Attention Deficit Disorders

As we saw above, this clinical picture corresponds to the 'too light' constitution type. When considering the following additional information it will become clear that the diagnosis of being 'too forgetful' (which is frequently overlooked) could also play a part here.

A) Either (1) or (2):

Attention deficit:

1) Six (or more) of the following symptoms of *attention deficit* to have been present for at least six months to a degree that is inappropriate and inconsistent with the level of development:

— Often not managing to give sufficient attention to details, or making careless mistakes in schoolwork, work or other activities: *too light, too forgetful, too closed* constitution types.
— Often struggling to keep the attention to tasks or play: *too light, too forgetful* constitution types.
— Frequently appearing not to listen when spoken to directly: *too light, too forgetful, too congested* constitution types.
— Often not following up on instructions or failing to finish schoolwork or chores or to fulfil obligations (not because of oppositional behaviour or inability to understand instructions): *too light, too open, too compulsive* constitution types.
— Having difficulty organizing tasks and activities: *too light, too forgetful, too heavy* constitution types.
— Often avoiding or having a dislike for or a reluctance to engage in tasks that require sustained mental effort (such as school- or homework): *too light, too forgetful, too closed* (sometimes), *too open* (sometimes), *too heavy* constitution types.

— Often losing items needed for tasks or activities (e.g. toys, homework, pencils, books or tools): *too light, too forgetful* constitution types.
— Often being easily distracted by extraneous stimuli: *too light* constitution type.
— Often being forgetful in daily activities: *too light, too forgetful, too closed* constitution types.

Impulsiveness
2) Six (or more) of the following symptoms of *hyperactivity* to have been present for at least 6 months to a degree that is inappropriate and inconsistent with the level of development:

— Frequent restless movements of hands or feet, or moving around on one's chair: *too light, too forgetful, too compulsive* constitution types.
— Often getting up off the chair in the classroom or in other situations where there is an expectation to remain seated: *too light, too forgetful* constitution types.
— Frequently running around or climbing onto things in situations where this is inappropriate (in adolescents or adults this may merely be caused by a feeling of restlessness): *too light, too forgetful* constitution types.
— Inability to play quietly or engage in relaxing leisure activities: *too light, too forgetful, too compulsive* constitution types.
— Frequently being 'on the go' or unable to stop: *too light* constitution type.
— Often talking non-stop: *too light* constitution type.

It becomes clear from the above that the 'too light' constitution type corresponds most closely to ADHD, and that this diagnosis may also be given to people with other constitutions.

Autistic Spectrum Disorder in relation to the constitution types

A disorder on the autistic spectrum is a psychiatric diagnosis, which, nowadays, is increasingly being given. This should not be surprising, because no one is completely in balance with themselves and their environment. Fully open contact is only possible once this balance has been achieved.

As soon as there is talk of a behavioural or developmental disorder it speaks for itself that there will also be a problem in the connection with the person's own thinking, feeling and will, in relation to self as well as to others. There will then not be any flow in one or more aspects of the contact and it becomes obvious that the person is unable to feel empathy with someone else. This phenomenon is sometimes called 'Theory of mind'.

The diagnosis of ASD can occur in any of the six constitution types, but most of all in the 'too open' and the 'compulsive' types.

In connection with the constitution types and developmental delay I would now like to turn to one criterion from the DSM-V, the international manual of criteria for diagnostics, namely to the qualitative limitations in social interaction: obvious problems in the use of different forms of non-verbal behaviour, such as eye contact, facial expression, body language and gestures as a way of determining social interaction.

In discussing this I will make use of the books, *Education for Special Needs* by Rudolf Steiner as well as *Children with a Difference* and *Children's Destinies* by Walter Holtzapfel, complemented by knowledge from my own experience.

The 'too compulsive' constitution type

Adults and children with characteristics of the *too compulsive* constitution show hardly any—and sometimes only fleeting—eye contact. One can also observe that they seem to look right through you. They often have a searching look in their eyes. Depending on their developmental level, their facial expression is not very lively, but static and rigid. Their posture is generally rigid and stilted and they hardly use any gestures for communication. Those with a 'too compulsive' constitution often develop their own ways of expressing themselves, both verbally and non-verbally.

The 'too forgetful' constitution type

Adults and children with a *too forgetful* constitution do not easily look into someone's eyes and some never do. Their facial expression can be very passive and at other times focused and enthusiastic. Their posture reflects their mood swings but it is not always easy to interpret what they want and mean to say. Some people with this constitution have hardly any or no social skills. They do not know their own name and will use gestures as an means to indicate what they want. Others may be quite sociable at times, but always in a superficial way.

The 'too congested' constitution type

Persons with a *too congested* constitution make an insensitive impression, as may be seen in the absent-minded, closed or rather coercive facial expression. When somebody tries to make contact with them their reaction will be barely visible, if at all. At other times they can show a lively interest. Their eye-contact makes a cool impression. They tend to either control social interaction or to exclude themselves completely. They tend to meet people who are in charge with demanding behaviour. Their posture strikes one as somewhat heavy and it is not easy to glean anything from it.

The 'too open' constitution type

Adults and children with a *too open* constitution are usually alert and hyper-sensitive. Impressions tend to enter them randomly. They either adapt to everything or refuse to join in. They have a poor self-image and at the same time they have difficulty accepting things from others. Their eyes are often wide open in fear and shock. When there is an incident or a row they will be watching closely, although they are unable to cope with it. They will cling to people who seem to be sure of themselves and who take the lead.

The 'too heavy' constitution type

The main problem for adults and children with a *too heavy* constitution is that they react slowly, but see a lot. They sometimes look into someone's eyes for a long time with great interest. They also enjoy making contact, but so slowly that the other person will have moved on or have lost interest. Their way of communicating and their level of thinking remain simple and concrete. Their posture can be recognized by its heaviness and slowness. Their movements lack expression. When put under pressure they may become very stubborn and nothing will get them moving again. As a consequence they may slowly fade into passivity.

The 'too light' constitution type

The type of person with a *too light* constitution will make eye contact with others, but not for long, unless it is in a quiet environment. They like to make contact, but their attention will be on other things very soon. The look on their face tends to express some kind of urgency and restlessness. Sometimes they flap their arms, expressing either fear or joy. They are helpful, but find it hard to concentrate, so things usually remain unfinished.

12
Diagnostic Methodology

Introduction

Anyone with a learning disability or a behaviour disorder is entitled to a regular diagnosis. Apart from this a diagnosis can be made in relation to the constitution type. A thorough physical diagnosis, preferably by a medical doctor, is necessary.

About the constitution types

A one-sidedness in any of the main functional areas can cause a wide range of physical and behavioural symptoms belonging to the area. Such a complex of symptoms used to be called a 'clinical picture'. Nowadays the term 'constitution type' is used, as this seems more appropriate in our time. There is a clear medical aspect to these 'pictures'.

It appeared to be impossible to describe for each constitution all the symptoms on all cognitive levels. The constitution types as described in this book are primarily related to children and adults with learning disabilities.

Determining whether a certain picture fits a child or adult is not simply done by ticking boxes in a checklist. It is good to first read the chapter in question properly and then compare it with the other chapters. A constitution is a complex of phenomena that are interrelated and flow into each other. The picture as a whole shows the way. Not all of the characteristics will be found in someone with a particular constitution and some are not exclusive to only one constitution type. Compulsions, for instance, can occur in several constitution types albeit for different reasons. After having obtained a clear image of the disharmony within the constitution (the three functional areas as a whole), the approach to that particular compulsion will arise out of it. This will prevent merely eradicating symptoms and/or correction of behaviour.

Observation checklist

Some time ago Hans Bom compiled the following observation checklist. This list is still being used successfully with some alterations. The four levels of existence belonging to this view of the human being are the basis for the first four lists of questions. The description of the items on this list can provide a *comprehensive image* of the person. The constitution type can be determined on this basis.

It is helpful to begin by posing a question you wish to research in relation to the person you are observing. The important thing is to mainly give descriptions, more about 'how' than about 'what', and to try and avoid words such as 'good' or 'weak' or 'better' etc.

1 Questions on the level of the physical body

— What is striking in the outer appearance?
— What can you say about the proportions of head, torso and limbs?
— What is the weight, the height, the age?
— Colour and shape of the eyes? Is the eyesight poor?
— The shape of the face, forehead, nose, cheeks, chin, mouth and teeth?
— Are there any special details in relation to hearing or any other senses?
— Hair colour; is the hair straight or curly, thick or sleek?
— Describe what you can observe from the nails, hands and feet, legs and arms, stomach and back, neck and head.
— Describe the person's movements; are they supple or rigid, fast or slow, jerky or fluid, heavy or light? Typical movements of legs, arms, hands or head? Any characteristic postures?
— Are there any obvious repetitive movements, such as nail-biting, flapping, fidgeting, rocking, rolling the head, thumb sucking, hitting oneself, scratching, head-banging etc?
— Are there any uncoordinated reflexes?
— Are there any particular movements this person can or cannot manage? Describe *how* they are made, for instance when running, jumping, skipping, hopping, standing still, sitting, cycling, roller-skating, swimming, walking etc.

2 Questions on the level of vitality and the life processes, the etheric body

— What is the general state of health?
— What about the vitality?

— Any use of medication? What is it? Are there any side effects?

— How is the endurance when climbing stairs, walking, cycling, swimming?

— How is the breathing? Is it deep, shallow, fast, slow, normal?

— What about falling asleep? Sleeping through the night? Waking up to go to the toilet? The average hours of sleep?

— What about warmth? Is there a perception of cold and heat?

— How is the blood-circulation? Are there any areas that are particularly cold, such as hands and feet, tummy, ears, nose?

— How is it with eating? Much or little? Are there any preferences for savoury, sweet, sour, bitter, or for bread, porridge, hot or cold meals? Any diet?

— What about drinking? Any preferences? Cold or hot?

— How is the secretion? Urine, stool, perspiration, saliva, any dribbling?

— How is pain perceived?

— Do minor wounds/illnesses heal quickly or slowly? How are the growth processes?

— Is the skin thick or thin, taut or soft, dry or moist?

— Is there any question of inflammations or rather the opposite?

— Is the medical history known? Are there any chronic diseases, epilepsy or anything else?

— Is there any hyper-sensitivity, e.g. to clothing, foods etc.?

— What can be said about the sexual development and about the primary and secondary sexual characteristics?

3 Questions on the level of the soul, behaviour and psychological functioning: the astral body

Always keep in mind healthy development when describing the following:

— What about daily activities, such as washing, toileting, physical care, brushing teeth, dressing and undressing, taking a shower, cutting nails, choosing clothes, fixing things, polishing shoes, tying shoelaces, doing buttons, doing up zips, tidying up one's room, cleaning etc.?

— What about speech: voice, sentence structure, pitch and modulation? Is there any stuttering, monotony, any unduly stressed syllables, any or no particular sounds? Is the speech slow or fast? Short, unfinished or complete sentences?

— How much does this person understand from what is said and how can you determine this?

— What do they understand about their environment? What can they do on their own without any support and when and how much do they need to be motivated?

— Is there any striking behaviour that leads to temper tantrums, withdrawal, screaming, shouting, being unusually cheerful, excited, compulsive, full of fantasies, doubt or any other form of behaviour? Is there even-temperedness or are there mood swings? Are they easily influenced or in control of themselves? How often in the day do these things occur?

— Is there sensitivity to stimuli from outside or from within? Do these stimuli have any lasting effect on this person or do they simply pass them by? Are they at the mercy of the environment or engage in it?

— Is there any imitation?

— Is there any enjoyment in learning and an ability to do so?

— How is the perception? Any possibility of making a distinction?

— Are there any fixations? Any fears, uncertainty, avoidance?

— Is there any sense of space and of time? An ability to make logical links?

— Is there any interest in the environment? Any sign of empathy?

— What is the approach to concepts? Are they interpreted literally? Any ability for abstractions?

— Are there any sympathies and antipathies?

— When does this person get stuck? How often does this happen?

— How is the relationship with peers and group leaders?

— Are there any friendships and how are they made?

— Are tasks easily done or is there resistance?

— Does the person show respect for others or are they impudent and rude?

— Do their actions make sense, compared to those of children/adults of the same age who have developed normally?

— Can they amuse themselves or are they easily bored?

— Can this person make plans and execute them?

— Do they have any hobbies or favourite activities?

— What is liked and what disliked? Is there any attachment to people or objects?

— Is the person domineering or docile?

4 Questions on the level of personal initiative and self-directed will: the 'I'

Always keep in mind healthy development when describing the following:

— How is content expressed through speech and voice?

— What about the posture? Is it upright or hunched?

— Do they say 'I' to themselves? Can they distinguish between 'I' and 'you'?

— Is there any ability to reproduce content from memory?

— Are they able to look forward to an event?

— Does the person have an overview of events in relation to time? From when and for how long?
— Is there any perseverance, any ability to cope with events? Any self-confidence, trust in other people, ability to put things into perspective, resilience, conscience? Any sense of one's own strength? Any insight into one's own deeds?
— Any ability to follow instructions for tasks etc. independently?
— Is there any ability to make one's own plans and take initiative? Is there any sign of courage, recklessness or anxiety?
— Is there a question of shame? How does it show itself?
— Any warmth for people or things in the environment? How is this expressed?
— Is the person flexible?
— Are there any special talents? Anything in which they excel or which is especially appreciated by others?
— Are there any ideals and how are they dealt with?
— Is the character balanced or fickle?
— What about spatial orientation indoors, on the premises, in town?
— Is the person able to deal with traffic?
— Are they able to travel on public transport independently?
— Can they use the phone independently?

5 Events in the past year

— Were there any important events at home, in the group, at school or at work?
— Were there any important physical changes, illnesses or hospital admissions?
— Were there any important events in their own lives?

6 Description of the person's typical strengths or weaknesses

— Name three strengths and three weaknesses of this person. Describe a characteristic situation with regard to a positive or worrying development.
— What is your assessment of their social-emotional level of development? Give age(s).
— What is this person's IQ?
— What is the official diagnosis?

Constitution type

Formulate a hypothesis with regard to this person's constitution type, underpinned by observations. Do not give a causal interpretation but one based on the whole picture.

Question

Look back at your initial question concerning this person. What progress, if any, have you made regarding this question?

Is there anything else you have discovered or understood and which you might want to work with at some point?

A combined diagnosis

It appears to be possible to make a diagnosis which includes both the regular clinical picture and the constitution type. In this way one could speak about a 'too open ASD' or a 'too closed MCDD'. Many combinations are possible.

Assessment in an outpatient clinic

Below you will find a model of an additional outpatient assessment, based on the work of Marijke Bijloo, a remedial educationalist in the outpatient clinic of the 'Zonnehuizen' in the Netherlands. This model was drawn up by Magrit Norde and Matti van Wifferen, a children's therapist and a remedial educationalist at the outpatient clinic of the 'Zonnehuizen'. This model comprises points for observation as an aid to determine the constitution type, among other things. Expertise is required in order to interpret the different observational data.

Assessment report based on anthroposophic remedial education

Name of client:
Date of birth:
Assessor:
Present:
Date of assessment:

First impression

First contact with assessor; saying good-bye to mother/father. How does the child come along with you? Observation in the waiting-room; handshake.

Outer Appearance

— Striking features. Proportion of height and weight, height and age; proportion of head-trunk-limbs.
— Shape of the ears (ear lobe shows will, mid-ear feeling, top of the ear thinking), head (forehead, hind head, shape of chin, width of head), nose, lips (in infants mouth in relation to sucking: lower lip relates to metabolism; upper lip to formative aspect). How strong are the formative forces?
— Shape of limbs.
— Any specific features of the hair.
— Skin (thin, thick, greasy, dry).
— Change of teeth.

Expression

— Voice—loud/soft, monotonous, restrained, pinched?
— Eyes—directed inwards or outwards, dreamy, sharp, expressive, dull, penetrating?
— Posture—upright, hunched, leaning forwards?

Contact

— Is there any mutual contact? Eye-contact. Openness or defensiveness? Any depth?
— How is the child's contact with you (dependent, wanting to be liked or self-willed)?

Motor skills

— Spinning tops. (Left-handed, right-handed, strength of fingers, good movements?)
— Yo-yo. (Do they sense when to pull it up and are they sufficiently in control? Children can usually manage this from the age of 7.)
— Kaleidoscope. (Eye preference, can they look with one eye while closing the other one? Let them name colours. Why can you see all these lovely patterns? Do they understand the mirror effect?)
— Jigsaw puzzles. (Is it trial and error or does the child see it immediately or suddenly?)
— Russian dolls (only for very small children).
— [Quasi-] tightrope walk. (Forwards and backwards, do they keep a straight line and retain their balance? Children should be able to do this from the age of 7.)

— Walking on their heels, forwards and backwards, walking on tip-toes forwards and backwards. (With young children: can they do it, do they get overexcited or do they fall?)
— Running. (How does the child move?)
— Hopping. (On the left and the right leg, forwards and backwards, which leg is the preferred one or which leg works best? Children should be able to hop on one leg from age 6,7.)
— Skipping. (Do they know what it is and can they do it?)
— Big ball. (Throwing underhand, overhand, with a bounce; hand preference, are they able to throw with one hand; how strong is their throw and can they catch the ball?)
— Small ball. (Throwing it over- and underhand, catching it with both hands and with one hand, throwing and catching it again straight away. Can they manage this?)
— Jumping exercise: sideways—putting the feet together, forwards or backwards—putting feet together, clapping hands at the same time. See whether the child can get into the rhythm (from the age of 8-9). Show them first, then let the child imitate it. Begin with jumping sideways—putting feet together. Then sideways—putting feet together, forwards/backwards—put them together. Then add the hands, clapping each time the feet are being put together. Watch the child's ability to pick up the rhythm (from age 6-7). Are they able to imitate? How do they experience their body? Are they able to integrate above and below. (From about 8 years)?
— Skipping with a rope. (Do they sense what is above and what is below? Children who are not well-integrated can only do this much later than usual.)
— School-readiness. Can they reach their ear with their arm over their head?
— Can they do finger-games (two ways: twirling their thumbs and 'Incey Wincey Spider', which they learn in nursery class)?

'Day-dream tree' (from about age 7, 8)

'Imagine a tree.' Most children can do this best with their eyes shut. Let them first sit down comfortably and then shut their eyes. Let them imagine a tree. Tell small children to draw this tree straight away and then ask questions about the tree. Children who prefer not to close their eyes can imagine a tree with their eyes open.

Ask about all of the sense impressions.

— Is the tree old or young, big or small?
— Does the tree have any leaves?

— What shape is the top?
— What colour is it?
— What does the trunk feel like (smooth, rough, soft, hard)?
— Where is the tree and what do the surroundings look like? Are there any other trees around it and are the trees touching?
— Can you hear any sounds? Are there any animals?
— How is the weather and what does the sky look like?
— If a child draws things in the tree, this will usually point to some kind of damage. Ask if anything has happened.

Introduce the image of a thunderstorm. A thunderstorm approaches and passes over the tree. Ask what happens next. Observe how the child deals with resistance. Always let the thunderstorm pass from left to right (from past to present).

Interpreting the data

Drawing
What do you notice while they are drawing?

— Is the child left-or right-handed?
— Do they sketch/ do they draw cautiously or with thick lines and much pressure on the pencil, open or dense, small or large?
— How does the drawing differ from the dream?

A conversation

— To start with, see whether the child can explain why they have come. If the child is unable to do this, let the parents explain it to the child and observe the child's reaction. In this way you will get a good picture of the interaction between parent(s) and child.
— Later on, during the assessment, have another conversation.
— Are there any siblings?
— Ask if they ever quarrel: often/sometimes, with whom? How is a quarrel resolved? In this way you can see how the parent(s) deal(s) with anger and resistance.
— Ask questions about school, teachers, school-mates and friends in the neighbourhood.

— Does the child play in friends' houses or vice versa; what do they do together and who decides?
— Ask about leisure time: what are the hobbies?
— How about eating, sleeping (falling asleep, sleeping through the night, waking up)?

Incomplete sentence test (Rotter)

Is the child able to complete her/his sentences easily? Are there any notable themes? Does the child talk about them?

Conclusion

Findings/the picture: look at the constitution types, characteristics of ASD, ADHD, symbiosis etc. What questions do these things call up in you? What needs special attention in the child review?

Advice

What is your support proposal (include anthroposophic therapies as well as other forms of support and therapy)?

Deliberations

Do not interpret separate components causally; they are part of the complete picture.

13
Practical Exercises for Educators and Support Workers

Introduction

The exercises in this chapter came about because of the subjects I was asked to turn to in workshops and lessons in various work situations. Most of the exercises came about by using a method called 'empathic observation' which is the second step in Goethean phenomenology.[30]

One way of doing this is the following:

Try and find out which new sensations you experience when imagining yourself having the main characteristics of a constitution type, such as: 'having a very thin skin'. We all carry all of the human possibilities within us (and therefore also any of the constitution types), although we only use a part of them. After having worked with these empathy exercises for a long time it has become clear to me that the point is not simply imagining yourself in someone else's skin. I think that it is a question of expanding one's own inner world of experience. I have come to the conclusion that by doing such an empathy exercise, through the indications that have been given when practising 'empathic observation', the boundary of one's usual experience is being crossed. By imitating the constitution of a person who is 'too open', for instance, one will be able to consciously experience and describe this constitution. The experiences will become clearer the more this is practised.

Exercise 1: Imagining/experiencing the constitution types based on the state of the physical body

Indications for imagining the different types

— *Too light:* Start by observing all that moves within your body (energy, warmth, flow). Then imagine that all of the fluid processes in your body are accelerating, causing you to be given up to them as they are so strong. You want it to be different.

— *Too heavy:* Start by observing all that moves within your body (energy, warmth, flow). Then imagine that all of these processes in your body are slowing down. You would want to do something about it from within.

— *Too congested/closed:* First observe your skin, from within and from the outside. Imagine your skin becoming thicker while there is someone inside who wants to come out and to do something (this is not the same as depression).

— *Too open:* Observe your skin. Imagine your skin becoming thinner. Inside there is someone who would like to remain within.

— *Too compulsive:* First observe the actual process of forgetting. Then imagine that you are no longer able to forget anything. Whatever you want to forget keeps coming back.

— *Too forgetful:* First observe the actual process of remembering. Then imagine no longer being able to remember anything, even though you would like to.

While doing this, try and become aware of any changes in the following:

— What do you experience physically? Legs, head, skin, breathing and other processes.

— Would you want to be touched or rather not? How?

— How do you experience your surroundings? Sounds, scents and smells, space, people and any other impressions.

— How do you experience the way you think, feel and act? Has anything changed from normal?

— How do you hear a question, and what effect has it on you? Different from before?

— Do you want to move when you feel that way, or rather not?

— What do you need and what you are longing for?

— What would be the best way for the support worker to approach you in such a situation?

— What is the greatest threat whenever you feel that way?

— What would you like to eat now and what rather not?

Exercise 2: Attitude and approach to and support of a constitution type based on the description in this book

Age: choose an age-group.
Level: choose a level of IQ and EQ (Emotional Intelligence).
Constitution type: choose a constitution type.

What is the central motto in approaching someone with this particular constitution type?

— Apply this motto to the following areas:

1. Physical care.
2. Distance/ Proximity.
3. Activities: play and hobbies.
4. Nourishment/ clothing.
5. Artistic activities: play, hobbies.
6. Tension/ relaxation.
7. Place at the table, in space.
8. Learning.
9. Punishment/ measures to be taken.
10. Touch.
11. Tasks/ small jobs—how and what?
12. In case of aggression/ resistance/ disobedience.
13. Social interaction.
14. In case of anxiety/ doubt/ passivity.

— Are you familiar with a situation in which you feel too…?
— When do you experience positivity towards this child/ adult and when negativity, irritation or anger?
— What is demanded from you when supporting this child/ adult?
— What can you or can you not offer this child/ adult?
— How can you bear to look at this person? What do you need so as to be able to do so?
— What could you learn from this child/adult?

Exercise 3: Characterizing a constitution type based on behaviour with the help of the description in this book

Age: choose an imaginary person.
Level: choose a level of IQ and EQ (Emotional Intelligence).
Constitution type: choose a constitution type.

— What is a person with this constitution type good at/ not good at?
— Do they prefer to be alone or with others?
— What makes them sad, angry, aggressive, rebellious?

— What do they like to help with and whom do they like to help?
— What do they experience as the greatest threat?
— For what do they long most?
— What kind of fantasies might this person have?
— What do they enjoy doing and what are their hobbies?
— In what kinds of situations will they refuse to do what you ask them to?
— Do they or do they not enjoy being touched?
— What jobs would they like to do?
— How does the person deal with peers/ support workers?
— Which traits of ASD does this person show, if any?
— How does this person feel physically?
— Do they enjoy movement and, if so, what kind?
— How and from what do they learn?
— How does the person understand and think?
— In what kinds of situations do you yourself feel that way?
— What is the greatest challenge for them and what would they like to learn in life?

Exercise 4: Observation role-play, one or several children

The observational components A, B and C may be divided among several observers.

This exercise makes use of conscious inner imitation. We always anyway imitate with our muscles the person we are observing and with our larynx the person to whom we are listening. This enables us to inwardly understand those we see and what we hear. A support worker who has already been observing a client so often that they got to know them via the process of inner imitation plays this client in the next exercise. Support workers are usually able to get into this mode quite quickly.

A) What can you see?

— Back, head, torso, arms, legs.
— Pelvic area, hands, feet, face.

While:

— Walking, sitting, speaking, looking, interacting, standing etc.

B) How does this person react to:

— Space, windows, light, objects?
— People, sounds…?

What do you see them do?

— Withdraw, blink, become rigid?
— Get into action, make gestures, speak etc?

C) How do they relate to the surroundings and to themselves?

— Posture: upright/ bent over; do they say 'I'?
— Distinguishing between 'I' and 'you', sense of time/space?
— Self-confidence, perseverance, insight into one's own deeds, taking initiative, interest, ideals, balance?

Only describe what you can observe.

Exercise 5: Creating indications for a supportive approach

For this exercise choose a partner who is observing a different constitution from yours. Both of you have half an hour. One of you will develop ideas about a constitution type. The other person may ask questions, but not make any suggestions.

1. Concentrate on the picture, the essence and the theme of the constitution type. Look within yourself. You might see a particular person in your mind's eye, which is fine, but do concentrate on your own inner being. The other person joins the process of concentrating on the constitution type.
2. Allow certain indications for the supportive approach to arise out of this concentration, based on the theme. Try and be quite specific.
3. Develop a number of these indications into concrete actions for in the classroom on the basis of the following questions:

    — How is your inner attitude?
    — How are you approaching the person (in reality or imagined)?
    — How would you ask them to do something?

— What would be a suitable task?
— How would you support this task?
— How would you round it off?
— Is there a suitable place in the class-room?
— Etc.

Exercise 6: Imagination in relation to a constitution type

— Let all the information you have now gathered in relation to the chosen constitution type pass by your mind's eye.
— Put this information aside for now.
— Concentrate on what is going on within you.
— Allow an inner space for an image to arise on the basis of the exercises with the constitution type while being aware that it is also a part of yourself.
— Draw this image or describe it (for instance in a poem).
— Do the same exercise with other constitution types.

Exercise 7: Empathy, observation and role-play for advanced students

Divide the group into teams of two people each.

1. Each team is given a constitution type which it will be exploring.
2. Try and answer the questions of exercise 3 with the help of the descriptions in this book, but not yet in relation to an actual person with this constitution (20 minutes).
3. Use the empathy exercises in order to imagine yourself in the situation of the person. Answer the questions in exercise 2 (20 minutes).
4. Take it in turns to move like this person. The other one observes and may give advice (10 minutes).
5. Take turns in setting each other a task. The one person is the client, the other the teacher/ support worker; pay special attention to the attitude:

   — How should this person be addressed?
   — How much space is needed?
   — What would induce the person to do the task?
   — What is not helpful? In your role as 'client' you are allowed to give hints:'It would work better, if you would do this and this…'

6. Discuss with the group about what does and what does not work for a particular constitution type; jot down the results (20 minutes).

Next step:

1. Role-play in the classroom or workshop setting: As 'clients' with the constitution type they have been working on the numbers 1 now join in a role-play of a classroom/workshop with several clients and someone on standby to take the place of the teacher/ workshop coordinator. The numbers 2 observe, (see exercise 4). The 'teacher/work coordinator' is appointed.
2. A classroom/workshop situation is simulated (choose a situation, age and level), arrange chairs and tables etc.
3. The 'teacher/ support worker' tells about their experience. The observers tell what they have seen according to the list of points for observation. The 'clients' tell what they have experienced.
4. Summarize. What have I learned? (Everyone taking turns.)

14
Case Studies

With gratitude to Ariënne Henkemans: the first four case studies about young people and their constitution types at a care-farm were written up in meticulous detail by her in her final project when training as a horticulture therapist.

Constitution type: too congested

Eric is a tall, strong, somewhat lanky young man with a mild learning disability. He is one of the residents on the farm, is engaged, eager to learn and will take initiative. In social life he is receptive, positive, and focused on people, but he does not like being in a group. In social-emotional and verbal skills his development has been delayed, causing communication problems especially when in a group, and it is hard to understand him.

Eric prefers physical activities and is proud of his (sometimes destructive) strength and endurance. His most important passions and interests are: fitness, physical work, stones and plants. In his contact with others, Eric could be characterized as a 'good-natured macho man'. He enjoys rough, heavy jobs (masculine, macho), such as moving heavy things and demolition work. On the other hand he can also be very quiet and gentle and he has an eye for details. Eric is energetic, enthusiastic, able to work hard and has a relatively long concentration span. He likes doing jobs that require muscular strength and shows great perseverance in getting heavy jobs done, but may at times exceed his physical limits. Afterwards he may then complain of having aches and pains and/or break one of the tools. He can also be aggressive and has a tendency to sneaky vandalism.

Obstacles and inhibitions

Eric prefers heavy and challenging work, but has difficulties with complex jobs, with the automatization of certain activities and with working at a greater speed. He dislikes fiddly work and struggles with small precision jobs that require the use of his fine motor skills (such as sowing, planting out, weeding etc.). He says that it stresses him out and that he cannot concentrate on it. Although Eric is able to do precise work he cannot muster enough patience or perseverance and is afraid that he will damage the plants.

Learning objectives

— Eric has to learn to channel his energy and at the same time to experience his own body (pain, tiredness and similar sensations) while not exceeding his physical limits.
— He will also have to learn to take better care of himself (personal hygiene, proper clothing).
— Developing his fine motor skills when caring for the garden is another learning objective for him.

Healing gardening activities

It is important for Eric to be able to do jobs in which he can use his energy, his need for physical exertion and his technical interest. Eric loves working outside in the garden and doing small jobs. He is also quite interested in working with machines (electric saw, file and other tools). When working with Eric it is very obvious that he has a preference for physical activity and likes to use and show off his muscles. His favourite subjects for conversation are his strength, fitness training and the weight of things he has dug out or moved. On the other hand it is also fascinating to see and hear how much Eric has already learned in the garden, what he knows about plants and their care and what he is able to do. He is good at observing the details in the garden and at memorizing names of plants and recognizing herbs and vegetables. It is good to pay positive attention to this side of him and to value and stimulate it.

Constitution type: too heavy

Umur is a young man of Turkish origin who had recently experienced a psychotic episode and on admission had been diagnosed with a type of schizophrenia with disorientation. This psychiatric problem caused a decrease in his cognitive powers from a normal level of ability to a mild learning disability.

Those around him (family and friends) as well as he himself are still in a process of becoming conscious of and accepting this change and its consequences. Umur is very receptive and sensitive to the atmosphere around him and to the mood of others. He is affected by these and is influenced by tension and relaxation and will copy the behaviour that goes with it. Umur receives medication to reduce compulsive thoughts and behaviour, such as asking the same questions again and again, looking at his watch, picking at things and fidgeting with his fingers etc. He shows these compulsive movements whenever he is anxious or stressed or afraid that something bad will happen. He needs much reassurance and affirmation. If he feels safe with certain people and is enthusiastic about something, he may also become over-excited when communicating and talk exceedingly fast (and intrusively), interrupting whatever is going on.

Obstacles and resistance
Umur is often restless and will complain of tiredness. Then he will try and avoid work and doing his jobs by talking too much, frequently taking breaks or going to the toilet. At work Umur is obsessively pre-occupied with the time, often looking at his watch. Then he is thinking about the end of work or of break-time and he can hardly concentrate on doing his work here and now. He is also easily distracted by passers-by, wanting to say hello to them or tell them something.

Umur has to watch his weight and move more, but it is difficult for him to be active at work and to motivate him to get moving. Umur is also hampered by nosophobia [fear of infections tr]. It is difficult to find out what his interests are, apart from resting, being at home and watching television. When alert and enthusiastic Umur will often talk very fast, mumbling unintelligibly.

Learning objectives

— To function steadily at work, concentrate and persevere (balance between working and talking).
— To learn to have an active attitude to work without getting too tired or having any pain.
— To care better for the garden, become more sensitive to the vulnerability of plants and learn how to deal with plants without damaging them (sitting on top of them etc.)

Healing gardening activities and development

Umur works in various areas of the care-farm and also attends class on several mornings. He only started work in the garden a couple a months ago. At first he did not want to work in the garden, because of his nosophobia and fear of getting his hands infected, but he has mostly overcome this. Now he will touch the soil and the plants without too much resistance and will put his hands fully into the soil and even work with horse manure.

Another reason for his resistance to gardening is his lack of familiarity with the work, the heavy physical exertion, and being outside, exposed to cold or heat. Apart from this there are not enough people working in the garden and there is always a lot to do, which demands that he is alert and prevents him from hiding behind others.

Despite these positive developments, Umur is always uncertain and passive when confronted with a new task and needs to be motivated and encouraged to fulfil it. His tiredness remains a cause for concern, and he frequently feels lethargic and unwell (due to medication or lack of sleep). Then he needs to be motivated to actively take up his work, to push a wheelbarrow, to move soil and plant herbs etc. He also needs to experience success and praise, otherwise he will become uncertain and nervous.

Whenever he understands what to do and is motivated to get it finished quickly (so he can have a break or go home), he is able to work quite fast (be it messily). It helps him to work step by step towards a clear aim, to give him breaks and to reward him if he has worked well. Umur is not yet very sensitive to the tender plants, their significance and uses. He may well be able to learn this if his interest for the nature of plants is stimulated. Given more inner peace, time and attention he will be able to learn the usefulness of his activities (sowing, planting, weeding etc.) and their purpose (beautiful and tasty products). His participation in selling plants at the local market might give him a greater awareness of the usefulness of his gardening work. The shared experience of the market has already had positive effects on him and woken him up. Within a couple of hours he changed from being heavy and tired, to being open and enthusiastic!

Constitution type: too light

Rob is a young man with a moderate learning disability and a relatively low IQ (48), attention deficit, hyperactivity and lack of concentration (ADHD). He is very eager to learn, is motivated and has a reasonably good memory. Communication is difficult for him and he speaks fast with poor articulation. Rob has a high pain threshold and is physically very restless. He is sensitive to the weather, to rain and storm etc. This tends to affect his mood and his behaviour.

Rob is fundamentally positive and enthusiastic. He also is an energetic doer, who does not just want to talk about things but loves to work. Because of his strong will, his desire to do things well, and his eagerness to learn, he accomplishes a lot. However, due to a short attention span he tends to stop halfway through, to work messily or be in too much of a hurry to finish his work properly. If he does not feel well, he will become impatient. He needs structure and regularity and is not very flexible. If told well in advance, he will be able to deal with changes in activities, plans and people. If he is not told, he tends to feel misunderstood and will get stressed out.

Obstacles and inhibitions

Rob lives in his feelings, and dealing with emotions is a challenge for him. He gives much importance to what people think of him and finds it hard to cope with negativity and criticism. He needs success stories and praise, but does remain himself. He likes working with his hands, learns quickly and will follow instructions, but if the work is too complex he will get lost in it. He prefers masculine jobs and working with male work-coordinators.

Learning objectives

— To alternate rough man's work with jobs requiring fine motor skills.
— To increase his independence, work on his own and finish off work properly.
— To spread his energy evenly during work.
— To fix his own mistakes at work.
— To learn to deal with feedback and criticism.
— To enjoy working together with others.

Healing gardening activities and development

Rob is one of the residents of the care-farm and has developed into an enthusiastic assistant-gardener, which gives him much pleasure and self-confidence. He enjoys working outside, has a lot of energy and is a hard worker. He is good at doing the tasks he is familiar with and will carry these out step by step and in a structured way. One of his regular tasks is cleaning the shop on Fridays. He is not good at precision work and improvising, but he will do much extra work spontaneously, such as tidying up and cleaning the work rooms, watering the plants in the greenhouses etc. He feels responsible and will see what needs to be done.

As he has to learn to work independently he was, for instance, given the task to plant bulbs in front of the canteen. He did this very well and nicely, mixing different colours. The result, however, was somewhat messy, like a moon landscape with holes and mounds, but he did take the initiative to remove the weeds first. He had reason to be proud of this job he had done independently.

Rob is very involved in his work and wants to get things done, even if he has to work a bit longer during break times etc. He works very hard and quickly, but is a little rough with the delicate plants, so that they sometimes get damaged with leaves or branches breaking off. Sometimes he will handle them too firmly or put them too deeply into the ground. He does care for the plants and means well, but he is often a bit clumsy. This can also be the case when he is selling plants at the local market. He is the best and the fastest salesman there, but needs to be reminded regularly to handle the plants with care. Trying to make him work more slowly and carefully remains a difficult challenge. He will learn from subtle instructions and will then correct his mistake, trying hard not to feel hurt.

Constitutional picture: too open

Debbie is a young person, who shows problems with processing information associated with PDD-NOS, as well as a 'disharmonic development profile'. Until the age of 17 she had been living at home, going to school from there, until a recent emergency admission because of temper tantrums and aggression. She has a higher level in speech than in deeds. As she has a language disorder she often needs others to help her verbalize her thoughts. Whenever too much is asked of her mentally and the pressure becomes too great she tends to become insecure and upset. Most likely this is the case at home. If she is in a structured and quiet environment she is able to think clearly and learn new things. Then she will show moments of cleverness, humour and creativity. Debbie tends to confuse fiction and reality. She suffers from fantasies, phobias and nightmares.

Debbie is short, stout and energetic. She suffers from an eating disorder; at the age of 12 she had anorexia nervosa, but now she is overweight. She is obsessed and preoccupied with food. Debbie's strong points are her ability to be positive, her willingness to learn, and her ability to react positively to compliments and to express herself verbally. As to behaviour, however, there are complications. She has trouble making contact and dealing with negative reactions and experiences. She rarely makes contact and, if she does, it is in a peculiar way, by shouting and making odd remarks. She has a tendency either to isolate herself or to seek attention by behaving provocatively. She will run away to avoid difficult situations. She will deal obsessively with certain matters and has a tendency to negotiate boundaries and rules.

Debbie tends to get stressed out in the absence of structure and overview. She also has difficulties with a lack of clarity in rules, plans and changes. She is insecure and finds it hard to assess social relationships and situations. She often feels lonely and worries that others do not like her. She has a tendency to be suspicious and to put herself into the position of underdog or victim. In a room with several people she will often hide her face in her hands.

At present Debbie is obsessed with boys. When she sees boys, she will try to attract attention by giggling, calling out loudly and using obscene language or touch. It is then very hard to stop her or tell her off.

Needs and support

Debbie needs support with learning to socialize with peers and with improving a positive self-image. Debbie could be helped by being given a clear programme and structure, including concrete instructions on how to behave and why. Apart from this she benefits from experiencing success and receiving praise. She feels well when she is liked and appreciated.

Debbie can work hard if she gets a lot of attention and affirmation. She also has the ability to work neatly, but needs to be reminded to not hurry and to concentrate, to take her time and pay attention to the task in hand. She does not have any fear of failure and will happily begin a new task, but needs praise.

Healing gardening activities and development

For a couple of days Debbie cooperated very intensively in the greenhouse and in the herb garden. She planted lavender plants in the herb garden, planted out mint seedlings, sowed lettuce in pressed peat pots and in boxes in the greenhouse. These spaces are suitable for her because they are mostly screened off without too many stimuli to distract her. This precision work is good for her and calms her down. Debbie will at first not feel like doing it. Apart from this, she suffers from lack of clarity in her routine and from transitions when being collected from and brought back to her residential group. Then she will find it hard to get going and to work with concentration. At first she will still be preoccupied with food, the time, going home, and with meeting boys, and will ask a lot of questions about these things. Especially when working outside it will take her a long time to manage to concentrate on her work and stop finding distractions, complaining of tiredness, headaches and other aches and pains when sitting on her knees while planting. With much input by her support worker it was possible to divert her attention, so she was able to concentrate on the task in hand and on the immediate surroundings in the greenhouse. She does, however, remain preoccupied by whether or not something is edible, and must be watched carefully to keep her from eating lettuce, herbs and even worms.

The work with the pressed peat pots and lettuce seed was especially fiddly. Debbie obviously found this quite difficult, but concentrating on the work was of benefit to her. Then she would do it well and systematically. It calmed her down and gave her energy. Also for her it was hard not to be too rough and push the seeds too deeply into the earth and/ or break the little pots. It became clear that in quiet and clear conditions Debbie is able to work well, learn quickly, cooperate, remember what she has been doing and also to calculate numbers and write reasonably well. Once she has got going she is a hard and fast worker because she can do things automatically (is able to multi-task). She works fast and continuously and will persevere, although the work can be a bit shoddy at times.

Case studies in a therapeutic setting

At the 'Zonnehuizen' [a residential home for children with special needs at Zeist, the Netherlands, tr.] several therapists work with individual children in a therapeutic setting. The supportive measures are tailored to the child in question, based on an anthroposophic approach. Here are some examples of the many possibilities. *Supportive measure* : External oil applications ('Einreibungen') by Arie-anne van Kalsbeek, a qualified nurse and therapist.

First case study

Tina, seven years old. Constitution type: 'too open'. Attachment disorder and challenging behaviour.

Supportive measure
Prunus oil application to promote relaxation and security by providing boundaries and enhancing her vitality.

Description
Tina has just turned seven. Her height is 1.21 m. and she weighs 22 kg.

Case history: Both parents have a deprived background and are unable to educate their children. Her father attempted suicide and her mother has a mild learning disability.

I had not seen her before and my first impression was of a slight, small, fragile, open little girl. All her features are soft and delicately shaped. Her hair is fair, thin and soft. Her skin is thin and transparent, yet feels taut. She has dreamy blue eyes. Her voice is high pitched and childlike. She seems to lack vitality. Her movements are quick and fleeting. Her breathing is fast and shallow. Her heartbeat is irregular and the pulse is weak, light and fleeting. Her lower back, hips, thighs and feet are very cold. She has considerable eating problems and does not manage to swallow her bread, but will save it inside her cheeks. She hardly chews her food but lets it melt in her mouth. She has a sweet tooth. Her stool is irregular and varies from very hard to soft. She is toilet-trained. Sometimes her skin can be quite clammy.

She does not go to school because she is unable to concentrate sufficiently. She makes a fuss about everything. She is sensitive to the atmosphere and to moods and will often look around nervously. If there are too many stimuli she may show compulsive or rigid behaviour. She may also show physical aggression in the form of scratching and biting.

Treatment

During the treatment she keeps looking around and raising her head. She says she enjoys the treatment. She says: 'My mother should learn this too.' She looks very pale and she has black rings under her eyes. She seems to be afraid of sounds. She is also afraid of illness and death. Her spatial orientation and her body-awareness are inadequate. She does not experience heat and cold sufficiently. She does not relax during the treatment and will raise an arm or a foot without being asked to. Her toes are rigid with tension. She tends to keep moving restlessly.

In talking she stumbles over her words. She seems to be quick and superficial, yet appears to perceive details very well.

She forgets many things, is unable to find the room she was in earlier, and forgets the story that was read to her. She needs visual aids for anything offered to her.

She copes well with the 'oil application', as well as with the 'swaddling'. She shows adaptive behaviour, but at the same time she is very tense and feels cold. At first she could barely tolerate being touched, because everything was itchy. She is not used to being touched in a healthy way.

After the treatment she is being swaddled tightly. After the first session I decided to change to Solum oil because I felt that she is much too open and loses her energy in the environment. Solum oil creates a boundary and, in a way, forms a second skin. The first objective was to provide a boundary and the second to enhance her vitality.

After three sessions her restlessness has disappeared and her breathing has become regular and deep.

We play games in which she has to say whether an object feels warm or cold. This helps her get to know her own warmth-organization. In the meantime she is tolerating touch quite well and seems to be able to enjoy herself. When the support worker collects her she notices blushes on her cheeks. Something is beginning to move!

Second case study

John, eight years old. Constitution type: 'too compulsive'. Attachment disorder and behavioural issues.

Aims and supportive approach:

Creating safety by setting boundaries and increasing body awareness. Reducing tiredness and improving vitality.

Full body Prunus oil application

Objectives: security, warming through, relaxation and healthy vitality.

Description

John is small and has dark skin. He appears much younger than his eight years. He has big, brown eyes and black hair, combed back with gel. His facial features are well formed out, his ears are oval and the earlobes are round and flat. The nose is thin and narrow, but wider lower down. His lips are full, the mouth is wide and often open. He has poor body-awareness. He has no notion whether he is warm or cold. He has cold dry skin, like sandpaper. His breathing is high up and irregular, very shallow and almost imperceptible. He walks on tiptoes. There is a lot of tension in him. He often has bruises and small wounds. When at home he usually soils himself and is incontinent.

John notices a lot. He often wants to take the lead. I can see an anxious, uncertain and restless boy with a negative self-image covered up by acting tough and with bravura. He is very restless, both verbally and non-verbally.

His thinking is scatty and he appears to have difficulty in distinguishing reality from fantasy. He suffers from mood swings. In school he is unable to concentrate. When he is offered some fruit juice, he will say: 'I prefer a beer, please!'

Supportive approach

This boy received external therapy over a period of six months. The first objective was to create a feeling of security. He received light massage treatment with Prunus oil. After four weeks the second objective was to enhance his vitality by means of Hypericum oil. After two months his vitality increased and his body-warmth improved.

After four months he was able to cope with a session of three quarters of an hour after which he would lie in bed sucking his thumb. He learnt to enjoy peace and security. His breathing deepened and his body warmth continued to improve. His restlessness decreased and he was able to indicate when he was feeling anxious. His body-awareness improved and he no longer soils or wets himself when at home.

15
Striking Differences and Similarities between Constitution Types

Some remarkable differences between the constitution types have been described below. This could be helpful in finding out the constitution type of a person. The degree to which someone behaves in a particular way remains individual. There are also many overlaps between the constitution types. Everyone is, after all, a complete human being with many different possibilities. The difference between the constitution types is that a particular set of symptoms is more prominent compared to so-called 'normal' behaviour.

The opposite constitution types are in obvious contrast to one another, but the secondary characteristics may have some similarities, as is shown below.

Differences

Too compulsive / too open

— People with the 'too compulsive' constitution tend to have quite dry skin, and may look older than they are. They have compulsions originating from mental pictures.
— People with a 'too open' constitution usually have moist skin that is often cold to the touch. Compulsions or fixations are caused by a lack of stability.

Too open / too light

— People with a 'too open' constitution tend to be anxious and often hesitant and to have difficulty in getting going.
— People with a 'too light' constitution will have already started something before they know it, will not see danger and tend to take risks.

Too open / too forgetful

— Those with a 'too open' constitution will usually be awake, cautious, alert and sometimes suspicious.

— Those with a 'too forgetful' constitution tend to be more dreamy, alternately passive and active and are trusting in a somewhat naive way.

Too forgetful / too light

— People with a 'too forgetful' constitution will usually be playful and alternately passive and active.
— People with a 'too light' constitution tend to be purposeful in their movements (always aimed at something different) and continuously restless.

Too compulsive / too congested

— Those with a 'too compulsive' constitution are usually detached; they tend to observe and check things out and to follow you around with their repetitive questions.
— Those with a 'too congested' constitution tend to claim attention and can have an irritating and 'draining' effect on others.

Too congested / too heavy

— People with a 'too congested' constitution may appear somewhat dark and brooding. They tend not to be helpful and have difficulty empathizing. When they feel well they may show a wealth of wisdom.
— People with a 'too heavy forgetful' constitution tend to be good-natured and full of trust. They are helpful and have a kind of 'automatic' power of empathy. They show great wisdom in observation and empathy.

Too compulsive / too heavy

— Those with a 'too compulsive' constitution are usually restless, alert and often anxious.
— Those with a 'too heavy' constitution have delayed reactions and may have a kind of restlessness that shows that although they want to do something they are physically unable to do it.

Similarities / overlaps

Poor concentration

— Too compulsive: whenever the compulsion becomes too strong.
— Too forgetful: often due to not being able to remember or to a poor sense of identity.
— Too congested: when there is congestion in the body.
— Too open: with too many stimuli and too much commotion.
— Too heavy: seemingly due to reacting slowly.
— Too light: due to physical irritation and hypersensitivity to stimuli.

Severe temper tantrums and aggression

— Too congested: due to increased congestion.
— Too forgetful: out of the blue, like an explosion and sometimes in a bizarre way.
— Too open: when forced to do something and when not knowing what is going on.
— Too heavy: when being hurried along all the time.
— Too compulsive: due to an inability to execute compulsions for a long time and due to too rapid change in the environment.
— Too light: when stopped in one's tracks.

High sensitivity

— Too compulsive: whenever the compulsion is overwhelming and there is a lot of stress.
— Too forgetful: due to an inability to remember something in spite of knowing that it exists.
— Too congested: whenever the congestion becomes too much.
— Too open: all the time, as it is the main characteristic.
— Too heavy: actually all the time, but not easily noticeable to those around them and only dimly to themselves.
— Too light: are sensitive but ignore it.

Compulsions

— Too compulsive: compulsions as main characteristic, stemming from mental pictures.

— Too forgetful: compulsions to prevent forgetting things.
— Too congested: compulsions and rigidity when there is too much tension in the body, also due to diminished consciousness.
— Too open: developing compulsions so as to retain one's footing in the midst of chaos and to counteract the fear of falling apart.
— Too heavy: compulsory repetition originating from a lack of overview and from slowness.
— Too light: as a means of structuring the surplus of movement.

Self-mutilation

— Too compulsive: head-banging (head-aches? pressure?); the compulsion to hit or bite oneself (etc.) after a shocking event, despair.
— Too forgetful: a search for the self.
— Too congested: extreme stress caused by congestion.
— Too open: physical pain distracts from emotional pain.
— Too heavy: when approached in the wrong way; out of frustration about not being able to get moving (biting hands).
— Too light: out of the urge to move or, alternatively, to counteract this urge.

Gifts / talents

— Too compulsive: order, faithfulness and conscientiousness.
— Too forgetful: enthusiasm, social competence, optimism.
— Too congested: wisdom, strong will, perseverance.
— Too open: artistic sense, sense of justice, integrity.
— Too heavy: trust, humour, helpfulness.
— Too light: helpfulness, readiness for action, optimism.

Notes

1   Rudolf Steiner (2014) *Education for Special Needs. The Curative Education Course.* Rudolf Steiner Press, Forest Row.

2   Cor de Bode and Hans Bom (1991) *Dubbel geholpen. Gezinstherapie bij zwakzinnige kinderen.* Vrij Geestesleven, Zeist.

3   Sellin, Birger: 1995: *I don't want to be inside me any more* Basic Books.

4   *Gewoon leven met ongewone handicaps. Effectief begeleiden van mensen met een verstandelijke handicap met de B2-methodiek.* Nelissen, Soest.

5   See also: *Helende omgeving* door Annemieke Korte, Brochure Zonnehuizen.

6   Holtzapfel, W. (1991) *Children's Destinies.* Mercury Press.

7   Bob Witsenburg (2009) *Gezondheid, ziekte en therapie.* Witsenburg, Haarlem.

8   Rudolf Steiner, *At the Gates of Spiritual Science*, GA 95, lecture of 28-8/1906, Dornach 1990.

9   www.hersenstorm.antenna.nl.

10 Claire Sylvia (1997) *Hart en ziel*, Luitingh-Sijthoff, Amsterdam.

11 Steiner, R. (2014) *Education for Special Needs, The Curative Course.* Rudolf Steiner Press, *London.*

12 Damiaan Denys en Femke de Geus (red.) (2007) *Handboek obsessieve-compulsieve stoornissen*, De Tijdstroom, Utrecht.

13 www.library.thinkquest.org.

14 Ch. Njiokiktjien (2004) *Gedragsneurologie van het kind.* Suyi Publicaties, Amsterdam en X.S.T. Tan (red.) (2005) *Dysfatische ontwikkeling. Theorie, diagnostiek, behandeling.* Suyi Publicaties, Amsterdam.

15 Steiner, R. (2014) *Education for Special Needs, The Curative Course.* Rudolf Steiner Press, London from lecture 5, (in part freely paraphrased as in Geertje's book).

16 Roos Rodenburg op www.pedagogieknet.nl.

17 Dr. J.A.R. Sanders-Woudstra, prof. dr. F.C. Verhulst, drs. H.F.J. de Witte (1995) *Kinder-en jeugdpsychiatrie.* Van Gorcum, Assen.

18 Holtzapfel, W. (1991) *Children's Destinies.* Mercury Press.

19 See also www.epilepsiefonds.nl, www.epilepsie.nl.

20 Soesman, A. (2000) *Our Twelve Senses.* Hawthorn Press.

21 Holtzapfel, W. (1991) *Children's Destinies.* Mercury Press.

22 See www.kunstomteleven.nl.

23 Thijs Besems en Gerry van Vugt (2008) '*Kwart over twee, maar ik wil niet*'. *Ongekende mogelijkheden voor autisten en geestelijk gehandicapten door stimulering van hun en ons brein.* Scriptum, Schiedam. They work with BEN-therapy (Basic Experience Network).

[24] Zie vele uitstekende artikelen in het tijdschrift *Balans* van het Centrum voor ADHD, en www.balansdigitaal.nl.

[25] From L.M. Pelsser, J.K. Buitelaar, H.F. Savelkoul, 'Is ADHD een (niet)-allergische overgevoeligheid? Een hypothese.' *Ned. tijdschrijft voor allergie*, 2009, 3, blz. 86-92.

[26] A good description can be found in the book by Geertje van Egmond (2007) *Bodemloos bestaan. Het Geen-Bodem-syndroom: problemen met adoptiekinderen*. Ambo, Amsterdam.

[27] Annejet Rümke (2004) *Verkenningen in de psychiatrie. Een holistische benadering*. Christofoor, Zeist.

[28] Algemeen heilpedagogisch leefklimaat, see M.H. Niemeijer en M. Gastkemper (2009) *Ontwikkelingsstoornissen bij kinderen. Medisch-pedagogische begeleiding en treatment*. Koninklijke Van Gorcum, Assen.

[29] For more information about this clinical picture, see Annejet Rümke (2004) *Verkenningen in de psychiatrie. Een holistische benadering*. Christofoor, Zeist.

[30] E.W. Baars (editor 2006) *Goede zorg. Ethische en methodische aspecten. Een antroposofische benadering van kinder- en jeugdpsychiatrie en zorg voor mensen met ontwikkelingsstoornissen*. Uitgeverij Christofoor, Zeist.

Bibliography

(NB: titles in bold script are available in English, tr.)

American Psychiatric Association (2000) DSM-IV-TR

Baars, E.W. (2008) *Antroposofische gezondheidszorg. De professionele ambachtelijkheid van gezondheid bevorderen.* SWP, Amsterdam

Baars, E.W. (editor) (2006) *Goede zorg. Ethische en methodische aspecten. Een antroposofische benadering van kinder- en jeugdpsychiatrie en zorg voor mensen met ontwikkelingsstoornissen.* Uitgeverij Christofoor, Zeist

Besems, T. & Vugt, G. (2008) *Kwart over twee maar ik wil niet. Ongekende mogelijkheden voor autisten en geestelijk gehandicapten door stimulering van hun en ons brein.* Scriptum, Schiedam

Bode, C. de and Bom, H. (1991) *Dubbel geholpen. Gezinstherapie bij zwakzinnige kinderen.* Uitgeverij Vrij Geestesleven, Zeist

Bode, C. de and Bom, H. (1999) *Niet meer op slot! Het doorbreken van impasses bij jongeren met een verstandelijke handicap.* Van Gorcum, Assen

Bode, C. de and Bom, H. (2008) *Gewoon leven met ongewone handicaps. Effectief begeleiden van mensen met een verstandelijke handicap met de B2-methodiek.* Nelissen, Soest

Bos, A. (2008) *Hoe de stof de geest kreeg. De evolutie van het ik.* Christofoor, Zeist

Bühler, W. (1983) *Het lichaam als instrument van de ziel.* Christofoor, Zeist

Denys, D. and Geus, F. de (eitors) (2007) *Handboek obsessieve-compulsieve stoornissen.* De Tijdstroom, Utrecht

Dosen, A. (2010) *Psychische stoornissen, gedragsproblemen en verstandelijke handicap. Een integratieve benadering bij kinderen en volwassenen.* Van Gorcum, Assen

Egmond, G. van (2007) *Bodemloos bestaan. Het Geen-Bodem-syndroom: problemen met adoptiekinderen.* Ambo, Amsterdam

Ferwerda, E. (1998) *Koude handen en koude voeten.* Heilpedagogisch Verbond, Zeist

Frith, U. (2009) *Autism. A very short Introduction.* **Oxford University Press 2008**

Glöckler, M. (1994) *Ouders en hun kinderen.* Christofoor, Zeist

Grauwel, R. and Nooij, G. de (2003) *Omgaan met een dysfatisch kind.* Garant, Antwerpen/Apeldoorn

Greenspan, S. (2009) *ADHD onder controle.* Uitgeverij Nieuwezijds, Amsterdam

Hallowell, E. and Jensen, P. (2008) *Opvoedwijzer ADD en ADHD.* Hogrefe, Amsterdam

Heijkoop, J. (1999) *Vastgelopen. Anders kijken naar mensen met een verstandelijke handicap met ernstige gedragsproblemen.* Nelissen, Baarn

Heydebrand, C. von (1985) *Childhood***. R.S. Press**

Holtzapfel, W. (1991) *Children's Destinies***. Mercury Press**

Holtzapfel, W (1995) *Children with a Difference***. Lanthorn Press**

Jongh, R. de (2009) *Breinfabels.* Contact, Amsterdam

Kirchner, H. (1978) *Die Bewegungshieroglyphe als Spiegel von Krankheitsbildern.* Freies Geistesleben, Stuttgart

Kliphuis, C. (2007) *De ADHD van André.* Sjaloom, Amsterdam

Köhler, H. (1997) *Over angstige, onrustige en verdrietige kinderen.* Vrij Geestesleven, Zeist

Korte, A. *Helende omgeving.* Brochure Zonnehuizen

König, K. (1986) *Heilpedagogische diagnostiek en epilepsie en hysterie.* De Zevenster, Driebergen

Lemmens, H. (2007) *Het elastiek tussen lichaam en ziel.* Andromedia, Middelie

Linehan, M. (2003) *Borderline persoonlijkheidsstoornis.* Zwets en Zeitlinger, Lisse

Lievegoed, B. (2005) *Phases of Childhood***. Floris Books, Edinburgh**

Lommel, P. van (2007) *Eindeloos bewustzijn.* Ten Have, Kampen

Marti, E. (1984) *The Four Ethers***. Schaumburg Publications**

Matze, Ir. M. (1994) *Typologie en voeding, de rol van het dieet bij het constitutiebeeld van het 'zwavel'-type en het 'ijzer'-type.* Louis Bolkinstituut, Driebergen

Mees, L.F.C. (1980) *Geneeskunde op de drempel.* Vrij Geestesleven, Zeist.

Meijs, J. (2012) *Puberteit. De smalle weg naar innerlijke vrijheid.* Christofoor, Zeist

Niemeijer, M.H. en Gastkemper, M. (2009) *Ontwikkelingsstoornissen bij kinderen. Medisch-pedagogische begeleiding en behandeling.* Van Gorcum, Assen

Niemeijer, M.H. en Hoekman, J. (2007) *Verhalen van autisme.* Van Gorcum, Assen

Niemeijer. M.H. (2011) 'Beeldvormende diagnostiek met het Instrument van de Kinderlijke Constitutie (IKC), in: Baars, E.W. en Bie, G.H. van der (redactie) *Health promotion: preventief en curatief. Naar een duurzame gezondheidszorg.* SWP, Amsterdam

Njiokiktjien, Ch. (2004) *Gedragsneurologie van het kind.* Amsterdam, Suyi Publicaties

Pelsser, L.M. en Buitelaar, J.K. en Savelkoul, H.F. 'Is ADHD een (niet)-allergische overgevoeligheid? Een hypothese.' *Ned. Tijdschrijft voor Allergie,* 2009, 3, blz. 86-92

Perry, B. & Szalavitz, M. (2009) *De jongen die opgroeide als hond en andere verhalen uit de praktijk van de kinderpsychiater.* Scriptum, Schiedam

Post Uiterweer, G. (2001) *Curative Education—Constitutional Pictures* (private Publication, Edeline LeFevre)

Rood, L. (1994) *Het boek Job.* Prometheus, Amsterdam

Sacks, O. (2011) *The Man who mistook his Wife for a Hat.* Picador Classics

Sanders-Woudstra, Dr J.A.R., Verhulst, prof. dr. F.C., Witte, drs. H.F.J. de (1995) *Kinder-en jeugdpsychiatrie.* Van Gorcum, Assen

Sellin, Birger: 1995: *I don't want to be inside me any more.* Basic Books

Schoorel, E. (1998) *De eerste zeven jaar. Kinderfysiologie.* Christofoor, Zeist

Sitskoorn, M. (2008) *Het maakbare brein. Gebruik je hersens en word wie je wil zijn.* Bert Bakker, Amsterdam

Soesman, A. (2000) *Our Twelve Senses.* Hawthorn Press

Soldner, G., Stellmann, H.M. (2007) *Individuelle Pädiatrie.* Wissenschaft liche Verlagsgesellschaft, Stuttgart

Steiner, R. (1987) *Manifestations of Karma.* Rudolf Steiner Press

Steiner, R. (2000) *The Education of the Child.* Rudolf Steiner Press

Steiner, R. (2010) *Foundations of Human Experience.* Rudolf Steiner Press

Steiner, R. Various Medical Lectures. Rudolf Steiner Press

Steiner, R. (1990) *Education for Adolescents.* Rudolf Steiner Press

Steiner, R. (2014) *Education for Special Needs, The Curative Course.* Rudolf Steiner Press, London

Swaab, D. (2011) *Wij zijn ons brein. Van baarmoeder tot Alzheimer.* Contact, Amsterdam

Sylvia, C. (1997) *Hart en ziel.* Luitingh-Sijthoff , Amsterdam

Rodrigues Pereira, R. (2005) *Stuiterend door het leven.* Inmerc, Wormer

Rümke, A. (2004) *Verkenningen in de psychiatrie. Een holistische benadering.* Christofoor, Zeist

Tan, X.S.T. (red.) (2005) *Dysfatische ontwikkeling. Theorie, diagnostiek, behandeling.* Suyi Publicaties, Amsterdam

Treichler, R. (1996) *Soulways.* Hawthorn Press

Tuinier, dr. S., Verhoeven, prof. dr. W.M.A., Panhuis, dr. P.J.A. (2000) *Behandelingsstrategieën bij agressieve gedragsstoornissen.* Bohn Stafleu van Loghem, Houten

Wing, L. (1998) *Autistic Children; A guide for Parents.* National Autistic Society

Witsenburg, B. (2009) *Gezondheid, ziekte en therapie*. Witsenburg, Haarlem

Zabern, B. von (2002) *Kompendium der ärztlichen Behandlung seelenpflegebedürftiger Kinder, Jugendlicher und und Erwachsener*. Medizinische Sektion am Goetheanum, Dornach

A note from the publisher

For more than a quarter of a century, **Temple Lodge Publishing** has made available new thought, ideas and research in the field of spiritual science.

Anthroposophy, as founded by Rudolf Steiner (1861-1925), is commonly known today through its practical applications, principally in education (Steiner-Waldorf schools) and agriculture (biodynamic food and wine). But behind this outer activity stands the core discipline of spiritual science, which continues to be developed and updated. True science can never be static and anthroposophy is living knowledge.

Our list features some of the best contemporary spiritual-scientific work available today, as well as introductory titles. So, visit us online at **www.templelodge.com** and join our emailing list for news on new titles.

If you feel like supporting our work, you can do so by buying our books or making a direct donation (we are a non-profit/charitable organisation).

office@templelodge.com

TEMPLE LODGE

For the finest books of Science and Spirit